C000183696

WALKS FROM THE
LEEDS AND LIVERPOOL CANAL

Leeds - the start of the canal

WALKS FROM
THE LEEDS AND LIVERPOOL
CANAL

by

MARY WELSH

Illustrations by

CHRISTINE ISHERWOOD

CICERONE PRESS
MILNTHORPE, CUMBRIA

ISBN 1 85284 212 1
A catalogue record for this book is available from the British Library

ACKNOWLEDGEMENTS

My special thanks go to James Swindells, Waterway Supervisor, and his staff at the Burnley operations base who gave me unstinting help; to Tom Ledwith, acting boats manager at Wigan Pier, who made my walk through the town so pleasant; to John Howarth, commodore of the Crooke Cruising Club, who offered me unlimited hospitality; to Jospeh White of Crooke Hall Inn, for his kindness; to Kevin and Diana Clutton of LL Cruisers, Heath Charnock, for exceptional generosity; to Keith and Christine Whitwell and family for their helpfulness; and to Alison Hewitt, the canal projects officer, Liverpool, who was so helpful on my last walk. Throughout the canal's length I met with unfailing courtesy from British Waterways staff.

Finally, thanks go to three other special people: to Maureen Fleming, who walked every step of the way, checking and researching as we went; to Christine Isherwood, for her glorious illustrations which make the book such a visual delight; and to Tom, my husband, for his unfailing support and advice.

ADVICE TO READERS

Readers are advised that while every effort is taken by the author to ensure the accuracy of this guidebook, changes can occur which may affect the contents. It is advisable to check locally on transport, accommodation, shops etc. Even right of way can be altered. The publisher would welcome notes of any such changes.

Front Cover: Illustration by Christine Isherwood

CONTENTS

PREFACE

I am delighted to be asked to introduce Mary Welsh's book of circular and linear walks that use the Leeds and Liverpool Canal as a spine. The canal has been in use since 1816 and, with its branch lines, stretches more than 140 miles, the longest in the country. The book covers every foot of the way along this glorious route.

British Waterways is constantly planning and reviewing the future of our canals to meet the ever changing demands. The days when most canals were used for transporting goods from A to B are, in the main, over. Now a new approach has evolved to allow all interested parties - including walkers, boaters, anglers and cyclists - to use the canals fully.

British Waterways believes all users should enjoy this varied, safe and interesting environment while respecting each other's activities. It has no magic pot of gold for renewing the 200-year-old canal structures, and so must maximise its resources with joint ventures. It aims to involve user groups, local authorities and voluntary groups.

Canal staff have changed and are more customer orientated. I like to think we are approachable and open to constructive ideas, and will adopt them if practical.

Good walking!

James Swindells
Waterway Supervisor

Long-tailed tit
in alder

INTRODUCTION

W here can you find
.... One hundred and forty miles of glorious walking
along an excellent continuous footpath, where there
is no chance of getting lost?
... A way that takes you through delightful woodland,
over hills and through dales, past banks of wild
flowers and beside hedges full of birdsong?
... A quiet track through the hidden parts of cities,
which shows much of our industrial heritage?
... A route that reveals superb 19th-century
architecture, goes below bridges decorated with
Gothic ironwork and past locks where the
engineering involves simple ideas on a very large
scale?
... A trail on which everyone is friendly - from newly
retired people trying out their first long-distance
path to local folk taking the dog for a walk and with
time for a chat?

Where? The Leeds and Liverpool Canal.

Britain's longest canal was constructed to provide a trans-Pennine
waterway linking the emergent industrial towns in Yorkshire and
Lancashire with the North American market via Liverpool. Work
began at the same time from both ends, in Leeds and in Liverpool, after
the first Canal Act was passed in 1770.

By 1816 the canal had been dug by men with strong muscles using
just shovels and working in mud in all types of weather. Reservoirs had
been constructed to provide water to keep these vital commercial
arteries open in times of drought. A winding route had been devised,
following contours, to avoid as many of the hills as possible. An
embankment that carried the canal at roof-top height had been built.
Tunnels and cuttings had been hacked out, often with great difficulty.
Well proportioned bridges had been designed to carry other forms of
transport over the cut (fortunately, because of the lack of modernisation,
these have survived unchanged).

Between 1786 and 1919 the Leeds and Liverpool made a profit;
between 1820 and 1850 it made a huge profit. In 1972 the canal ceased
operations after the last barge of coal was delivered to Wigan power

station. Today it is still open along its entire length, providing a grand highway, with something different to see at every twist and turn.

Each walk starts from a point where there is suitable parking. Most are circular walks, using the waterway as a spine before or after exploring the glorious countryside through which it passes. A few are linear walks, and ideas on return transport have been included. The canal is well served by bus and rail and some walkers will want to forgo the lovely countryside and remain on the towpath to walk the entire 127- or-so miles - with no deviation.

For most of the walks, when the route takes you away from the towpath, strong shoes or boots are needed. Safety precautions should be taken, such as carrying waterproofs, whistle, food and drink and the relevant map. British Waterways advise youngsters to be water-wise by spotting the dangers - never go on ice, keep away from locks, never swim in the canal.

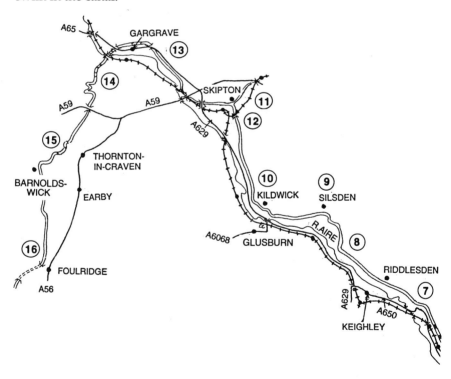

KEY TO MAPS

Canal with towpath			Lake, pond or reservoir
Canal with locks			
Canal with bridge			Built-up area
River			Deciduous woodland
River with weir			
M65 Motorway			Coniferous woodland
Dual carriageway with roundabout			Park
Major road			Churches
Minor road			Cutting
Track			Embankment
Path			Marsh
Railway			Golf Course
Railway with station			Trig point - hill summit
Railway with major station			The route
Disused railway			P car parking

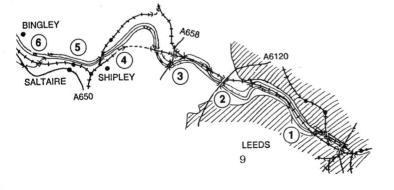

BINGLEY
6 5
SALTAIRE SHIPLEY 4 3
A650
A658
A6120
2
LEEDS 1

9

Crane, Leeds

Walk 1: Linear walk from Leeds basin to Kirkstall

Distance:	4 miles
Time:	2-3 hours
Map:	OS Pathfinder 683 SE 23/33 Leeds
Terrain:	Easy walking all the way. Towpath can be muddy after rain.

This is a linear walk. You can of course return by the same route, or you can take the bus back to the centre of Leeds, where the walk begins.

Leave City Square and walk down Bishopgate Street, with British Rail on your right. Pass under City House and take the second stone-lined archway on the right side of the road, signposted Granary Wharf. Continue along the vaulted way. Cross the bridge over the raging Aire and look right again to see the dark vaults that edge the hurrying water - a very dramatic corner of the city.

Beyond the bridge, turn left and walk ahead through the car park to the first lock on the Leeds and Liverpool Canal, which links the waterway with Aire-Calder Navigation. The ground about the cut, once the commercial centre of the city, has now been landscaped and there are grassy flat areas, seats, trees and several small cafes and restaurants. Look for the nineteenth-century wharfside crane, counter-balanced by a huge block of gritstone.

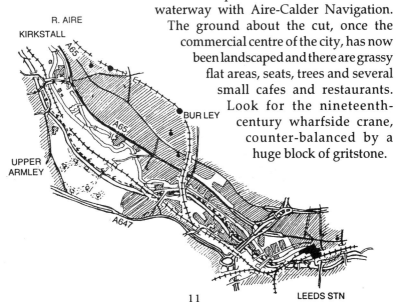

Walk the towpath of the canal, following the signpost for Armley Mills, to pass on your left Office Lock Bridge (226). It is ornately decorated and must have pleased those directors of the canal who passed it when they attended meetings in the company office in the 1770s. Beyond the canal office you can see two elegant and, at first sight, extraordinary campaniles rearing upwards. The one with the octagonal top was designed to extract smoke and the other iron dust from the manufacturing processes in Tower Works below.

Continue along the towpath to pass a second lock and then walk beneath a railway bridge. Beyond, black-headed gulls fly over the willow-lined River Aire, which comes close to the path. Stroll on along the quiet way to pass under several more bridges and beside St Ann's Ing lock (3), where the canal is raised 4ft 5$^{3/4}$in.

Look left to see Castleton Mills, built in 1838, with its great semi-circular stair tower facing towards you. Nearby is Oddy locks (4-5), which raise the canal 13ft 7in. Stride on past Spring Garden locks (6), where the canal rises 9ft. Now the towpath runs high above the River Aire, with a fine view over Leeds and its many church spires and mill chimneys.

Head on towards the splendid Leeds and Thirsk railway viaduct, which crosses the Aire valley. Pass under the canal arch, which is attractively ornate. Beyond the Canal Road Bridge (225A), which has an iron balustrade retained from the original bridge built in 1882, the pleasingly restored towpath leads to the side of Armley Mills, the Leeds industrial museum. Here you may wish to view the galleries showing many features from days gone by. (It is closed on Mondays.) Stride on to the end of the mill wall to see the spectacular mill dam.

Walk the towpath to pass under the metal bridge that carries the Leeds and Bradford railway over the canal, then continue to climb a low concrete bridge. Beyond, the towpath is flanked by water on both sides. On the right is an arm of the water, with metal bollards on each bank. These acted as moorings for coal barges servicing Kirkstall power station. Cross a second concrete bridge and stride on along the peaceful way, with the golf course and Gotts Park on the far bank. In the trees about the waterway look for blackbirds, long tailed tits, robins, wrens and pigeons. Alders line the canal bank and these are now adorned with plump reddish catkins.

Pass under Wyther Bridge (223) and continue to Kirkstall Brewery Bridge (222) before which you turn right. Walk up Bridge Road and continue over Kirkstall Bridge - a three-arched iron bridge - over the River Aire. Stride on to the A65 (Kirkstall Road), where you can catch the 736 bus to return to the city centre.

Walk 2: Circular walk from Calverley via Kirkstall

Distance:	7 miles
Time:	3-4 hours
Map:	OS Pathfinder 683 SE 23/33 Leeds
Terrain:	Easy walking all the way.

L eave the A65 at Low Fold roundabout, in the western suburbs of Leeds. Drive south-west along the ring road and park in the parking layby on the left. Walk down the road to pass over the railway. Cross the busy road with care and stride down Calverley Lane until it swings right. Walk the path that leaves the lane and cross the footbridge over the river. Bear left, following the waymark, to the side of the canal. Walk left along the quiet towpath, with the canal to your right. Pass under Horsforth Road Bridge (216A) and continue past Rodley swing bridge (217) and Rodley boat centre. Beyond, look across to Rodley, an attractive stone-built village. Continue past the crane works, today deserted but with its tall square chimney standing proud.

Stride on, now with the Aire coming close to the canal after the river makes a large meander. Trees line the banks of the cut and from these come the cheerful whisperings of small birds. Redwings, the sides of their breasts suffused with a rich pink, feed ravenously on hawthorn berries. Pause to enjoy the classical facade of Whitecote House, an elegant Georgian dwelling built of local sandstone, that edges the south bank of the waterway. Continue past Newlay locks (11-13), which have

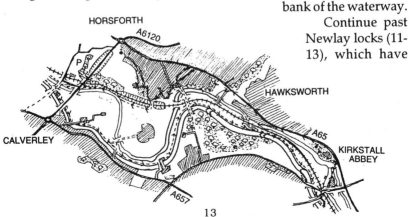

HORSFORTH

A6120

HAWKSWORTH

A65

CALVERLEY

KIRKSTALL ABBEY

A657

13

Kirkstall Abbey

Newlay Bridge - a very old iron bridge just off the path at Newlay, well worth stepping aside to look at

four sets of wooden gates. On the opposite bank the magnificent woods of Bramley Fall are criss-crossed with inviting paths. Stroll the towpath to pass Forge locks (8-10), which also has four sets of gates. Here a kingfisher flits from the stonework of the lock to the bushes on the banks of the Aire. Look left across the pastures to the dark outline of Kirkstall Abbey. Pass under Kirkstall New Road Bridge (221A) and continue, passing Kirkstall brewery on the right. Beyond Kirkstall Brewery Bridge (222) bear left, following the waymarks, to cross the road and walk Broad Lane.

Follow the waymarked busy road over the railway and the Aire. Cross the road and take the track leading off into parkland beyond the war memorial. This way, opened in August 1992, leads to Kirkstall Abbey, enabling walkers to avoid the busy A65. Enjoy the glorious Cistercian abbey, founded in 1152, with its spectacular tower and magnificent cloisters.

Join the A65, alas, and walk west for nearly a mile. Just after you have passed Hawksworth Wood on the right side of the road, look for the public bridleway sign on the left. Follow the wide track beside a wall on your left and the trees of The Outwood to your right. Continue along the track as it swings right, now welcomingly close beside the surging River Aire, to come to a narrow road. Walk ahead and then turn right to climb away from the bridge over the river. Take the second turn on the left to walk Newlay Grove and walk ahead to a footpath, left, waymarked with a yellow arrow with a red centre, to cross the railway.

Bear right. From now on the walk is waymarked and sheer magic, passing through pastures and beside the tree-lined Aire once more. Pass under the ring road and continue until you reach the footbridge you crossed at the start of the walk. Turn right away from the bridge and then right again to walk to the ring road. Turn left to rejoin your car.

Viaduct over the River Aire

Walk 3: Circular walk from Low Green, Leeds

Distance:	5¹/₂ miles
Time:	2-3 hours
Map:	OS Pathfinder 683 SE 23/33 Leeds 682 SE 03/13 Bradford
Terrain:	Easy walking all the way.

There is parking space for a few vehicles close to the old Friends' School in Low Green Lane just off the A65 at Rawdon. Continue along the short lane and walk on down the reinforced path, Cliff Lane. The path is hedged and passes through pastures. At an intersection of tracks, stride ahead through trees to descend steps to a narrow lane, where you turn left. Walk past The College and take a signposted footpath on the right just beyond the boundary wall of the pleasing building.

Follow the way as it swings left to pass through oak and holly woodland. Cross over an unmade lane and continue downhill along another with a notice saying "Private road, footpath only". Stride the track, passing Rawdon sewage plant to your right. Watch for your first glimpse of the Aire and take a narrow path (easy to miss) on the right

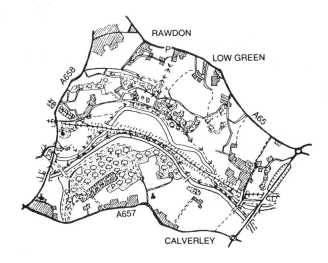

Kingfisher about to dive

before a fence, at the end of which there is a gap. Beyond, a good path passes through willows beside the lovely river.

Cross a footbridge over a feeder stream and continue past the Sandoz factory. Pass through a stone-arched tunnel and then under the railway bridge to a stile beside the Aire. Stroll across the pasture to another stile. Beyond, turn right to cross a cobbled footbridge (crossed in Walk 2) over the hurrying river where mallards have already paired. Climb the steps ahead and walk right to come to the side of the Leeds and Liverpool Canal.

Turn right, passing Owl swing bridge (216) and walk along the towpath where a kingfisher fishes. It perches on the canal banking and dives into the water with a considerable splash. Its electric blue back and rich red-brown chest lighten the dullness of a misty morning. Its short rounded wings beat faster and faster until they appear as a mere blur. Continue past Calverley Lodge swing bridge (215) and Lodge Wood.

Look for swans, moorhens, fieldfares and jays, all of which are seen along the way. Soon the towpath comes close above the Aire and then passes a colourful collection of narrow boats moored on the opposite bank. Pass under Thornhill Bridge (214B) and continue to Apperley Road Bridge (214A) after passing Barratt's shoe factory on the left.

Climb the steps to the right just before the bridge and turn right to walk along the busy A658. Cross the bridge over the Aire and take the signposted footpath on the right. Pass to the left of a clubhouse. As you approach the access track to a school, follow the footpath sign directing you right. At the riverbank, walk upstream along the edge of playing fields.

Continue below the four-arched viaduct and stroll along the riverbank. Watch out for the unmarked walled path that leads left uphill, below a row of fine sycamores. Take it and pass Underwood Grange to the right and walk uphill through another walled track. At the lane that edges Crag Wood, turn right, to take the stepped path through the wood that you walked earlier. Continue up the walled way, Cliff Lane, to regain your car.

Cobbled bridge over the Aire

Dobson Locks, Apperley

Walk 4: Circular walk from Apperley road bridge via Fox Bridge, Shipley

Distance:	8½ miles
Time:	4-5 hours
Map:	OS Pathfinder 682 SE 03/13 Bradford (W Yorks)
Terrain:	Level walking. Walk with care along the bank of Aire.

L eave Leeds by the A65 and turn left onto the A658 at the roundabout at Rawdon. Cross the railway and the River Aire and turn immediately left into Parkin Lane. Take the left branch where the narrow lane divides and park on the right at the edge of West Wood. Walk back to the A658, turn left and walk to the start of Apperley road bridge. Drop down steps to the towpath and pass under the bridge (214A) to walk through the quiet countryside, where swans swim to the side of the path hoping to be fed and then continue with their courtship rituals.

The towpath now comes to Apperley swing bridge (214) and its charming stone buildings and cottages. Here Dobson locks (14-15) raise the canal 23ft 8½in. This is a pleasant area where you can sit on a rustic

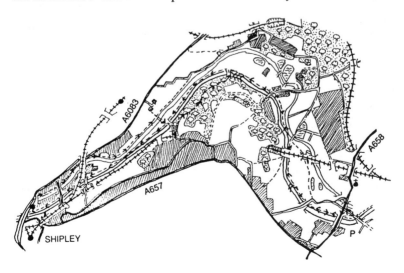

seat and watch the boats negotiate the fall in the cut. The towpath has been reinforced and the steps and paved way about the gates pleasingly restored.

Continue along the lovely way, where you could see a kingfisher flitting ahead from bush to bush. Carry on past Field locks (16-18), which raise the canal 25ft. Look right to see a spectacular viaduct spanning the valley. Enjoy the woodlands, Buck Wood, on the far bank where a pair of jays call raucously, keeping close together.

At the end of the extensive woodland you pass Buck Hill swing bridge (211). Look right here to see a very long iron footbridge that crosses the River Aire. Note this point for your return route. Stride on along the path, where elder bushes are clad in tiny pale green leaves, towards Shipley. Beyond bridge 209A, notice the milestone which says that you are now $12^{1}/4$ miles from Leeds and 115 miles from Liverpool.

Milestone

Head on past Dock Lane swing bridge (209), where mill walls crowd the banks, and then beneath the graceful stone Junction Bridge (208), which supports a cobbled way - you feel at any moment you will hear the clacking of clogs coming from above.

Leave the towpath at Shipley Bridge (207C), also named Fox Bridge after an old public house of the same name that used to stand close by. The path bears right to pass in front of a large shop selling bicycles. Walk ahead along the noisy road to cross Baildon Bridge over the River Aire. Take the signposted public footpath, which leads off right and winds, right, round Shipley Timber. Then concrete steps on your left lead you to the side of the Aire.

Here a decision needs to be made. For the next three-quarters of a mile the footpath, on your right, teeters along the edge of the fast flowing water. On your left steep factory walls come to the edge of the mostly paved way. Where the path passes bushes, trees and shrubs these have been cut back and it is well walked. But if you are afraid of

Pair of jays

walking close to deep water, turn back and return along the canal to the swing bridge (209) mentioned earlier.

Those who are happy to walk the footpath should climb the steps to cross a narrow road and then drop down more steps to the continuing path. Alders heavy with catkins and willows trailing branches in the water line the banks, but these do not hide the litter that despoils the high banks on which much of Shipley's industry perches. Negotiate with care the way beneath a huge stone viaduct where some of the banking has slipped away. Beyond, the path continues with a huge retaining wall close on your left and the deep, surging river on your right.

And then the path carries on, lined with bushes on both sides, and leads out to a more open area where a factory making radiators has pleasingly landscaped the riverside. Climb the stile and walk on to cross the long iron bridge (erected 1889) that spans the Aire. Beyond walk ahead up the paved slope and over the swing bridge (211) athwart the canal. Continue up the slope ahead to take concrete steps that ascend into Buck Wood.

Follow the track as it swings right and just before it reaches a tarmacked road turn left and walk beside a wall on your right through glorious woodland. Over the wall lies open ground. Once beyond this you quickly reach a wider track. Here turn left and walk the lovely way, in some parts lined with heather, beneath birch, oak and beech. The track continues for nearly half a mile and then descends gradually to Stangford Bridge (211) over the canal. Cross and drop down to the towpath. From here retrace your outward route, where you might see the kingfisher again still busily fishing.

Saltaire

Walk 5: Circular walk from Saltaire via Shipley

Distance:	2¹/₂ miles
Time:	2-3 hours
Map:	OS Pathfinder 682 SE 03/13 Bradford (W Yorks)
Terrain:	Easy walking

Drive west along the A6038 and turn right before Baildon Bridge into Green Lane, following the sign for Shipley Glen Tramway. Keep parallel with the River Aire and the Leeds and Liverpool Canal and at Baildon, where the road swings right, continue ahead along Coach Road for half a mile, passing the Cup and Ring public house. Park on the left beside a triangle of grass close to the entrance to Roberts Park.

Enter the park and walk along the terrace, where flowerbeds full of pansies or roses and variously coloured shrubs pleasingly form a border, to view the statue of Sir Titus Salt, mill owner and philanthropist. The statue was erected in 1903 to commemorate the centenary of Salt's birth. Look for the two plaques, one showing an alpaca goat (llama) and the other an angora goat; the fibres of both animals were used in the manufacture of material in Salt's mills.

From the statue view the extensive grounds of the park given to Bradford by Sir James Roberts as a tribute to the work of Salt. From here too you can see the extensive six-storey Italianate mill with its campanile, hiding a chimney, where Salt provided healthy working conditions for

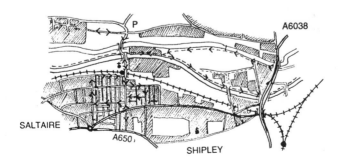

Almshouses, Saltaire

his huge work force. He built where he had efficient transport - the canal and the railway - for importing his wool and for exporting the finished product. The river washes the side of the mill and here the picturesque weir once provided water power for the works. Salt then built the village close beside the mill, naming it Saltaire and so combining his name with that of the river.

Leave the park and cross the footbridge over the river to explore the model village. Continue over Saltaire Bridge (207A) across the canal and walk up Victoria Road. Here on the right, opposite the works, the elegant United Reform Church stands aloof in its own grounds. Further along the road you pass, on your right, the works dining room, where workers and visitors could eat breakfast and dinner.

Continue up the gently climbing road to cross Caroline Street, named after Salt's wife, into Victoria Square. Here stands the magnificent institute, with ornate topped pillars and parapets, carvings round doorways and, over the main entrance, the Salt coat-of-arms. Here he encouraged his workpeople to read, to use the smoking room, gymnasium and billiard room. These he felt would fill their leisure hours and keep his workers from drinking, and therefore the village had no public house. Today the imposing building houses the public library and information service - and there is still no public house.

Opposite the institute stands the school, equally ornate and attractive, which once educated the 700 or more children of the village. The two buildings are flanked by four sculptured lions, each with its own expression and pose, and similar to those found in Trafalgar Square. The school and the dining room are today all part of Shipley College.

Continue up Victoria Road to see the charming almshouses provided for the old and infirm. These are equally ornate and are set back behind a green with shrubs and two graceful weeping willows. Look for the plaque in the porch of number 38, listing the names of the early occupants, giving their ages and the date of their taking up residence and of dying - a moving record. On the opposite side of the road, below more almshouses, stands the hospital, now a residential home.

Return along Victoria Road to turn left into Titus Street and walk its full length to reach Albert Road. As you go notice the dwellings built by Salt so that his workers could live in decent conditions. Some are very simple and plain, some are bigger and have small gardens and others are even grander. These variations relate to the jobs done by the occupants in the works. Turn right into Albert Road and look over the church and up to the hills above the village - a far cry from the smoke and dirt of the city from where Salt had removed his workers.

Turn right again to walk the cobbled Albert Terrace, which runs beside the railway, little changed from Salt's day. Turn left to walk past the dining room and then the church to cross the canal bridge. Turn left to join the towpath and walk left to pass below bridge 207A. Continue ahead with Saltaire Mill on either side. Stride on along the towpath, past the waterbuses at Shipley Wharf which in summer provide pleasant trips to Bingley. Continue until you reach Fox Bridge (207C), where you leave the canal. Walk north along the busy A6038 and take the signposted footpath at the start of Baildon Bridge to walk west beside the River Aire. This well maintained wide path takes you beside the tree-fringed river where blackbirds, robins, mallards, pied wagtails, moorhens and black headed gulls enjoy the quiet waterway.

After half a mile the riverside path joins the towpath close to the Saltaire Mill. Continue to pass under bridge 207A, where you leave the path to regain your car.

Moorhen

27

Packhorse Bridge, Beckfoot

Walk 6: Circular walk from Saltaire via Bingley

Distance:	6¹/₂ miles
Time:	3-4 hours
Map:	OS Pathfinder 682 SE 03/13 Bradford (W Yorks)
Terrain:	Easy walking all the way. Muddy in parts after rain.

Park as for Walk 5. Cross the bridge over the River Aire and continue ahead to the side of the towpath. Turn right, away from Sir Titus Salt's magnificent mill at Saltaire and Saltaire Bridge (207A), and begin the lovely walk towards Bingley. On the opposite bank stands the United Reform Church, built by Salt and, beyond, many allotments, originally provided by the mill owner for his workers to grow their vegetables. From here you can also see the houses of Albert Road, larger than most in the village. These were provided for the managers and overseers.

Stride on past Hirst loch (19), where the waterway is raised 10ft 2in. Beyond, on the far bank, is Hirst Wood, with tall beech and oak. On your right the River Aire comes close beside the canal, 10ft down a sloping bank. Blackbirds, blue and great tits, robins and wrens are busy with their courtship and a pair of swans come close, hoping to be fed.

On reaching the seven-arched Dowley Gap Aqueduct, do not cross, but drop down the slope to a footpath beside the alder-lined river. Walk

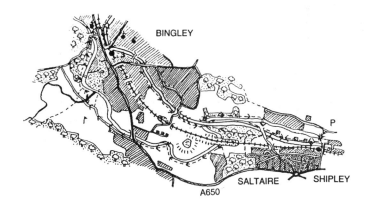

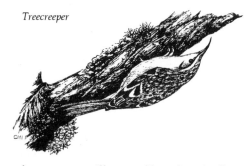

Treecreeper

ahead and then pass beneath the second arch on a cobbled way. Follow the narrow footpath beyond. Ignore the footbridge and continue along the path, now with the surging Aire to your right. Stroll through the southern slopes of the delightful Hirst Wood, where pussy willow and hazel are in flower and two pairs of jays court noisily, disturbing a mistle thrush which flies off "churring" angrily.

Pass below the railway bridge, where elder is in leaf. Moorhens swim from one bank to the other and race off into the bushes, at home on land as in the water. Look for a tree creeper busily probing the bark of an alder for unlucky overwintering insects. Continue along the path, which edges the river where it now makes a large curve in its course. The path then continues between high walls below Bankfield Hotel and then passes through a metal gate to a pasture. At the far end is another gate into more pleasing woodland where butterbur flowers.

Keep beside the river, as instructed by a notice, to walk beside extensive playing fields. Do not cross the footbridge but walk on along the now tree-lined way to pass to the left of a turreted aqueduct, built in 1897, carrying water from the Nidd valley. Stride on to the road bridge to cross, with care, the busy A650. Continue along Beckfoot Lane, with glimpses through the trees to the wide river below. Stroll on along the narrow lane, with the golf course to your left.

Ignore the footpath to the right and continue to Beck Foot. Pass the stone mullioned house, named Illingworth, and cross the cobbled packhorse bridge over Harden Beck. This, very shortly, empties its waters into the Aire. Pass through the gap stile on the right and follow the path, which keeps to the side of the stream. Then walk left beside the Aire. The path climbs steadily and passes immediately behind an attractive house. Beyond is a gap stile that leads into oak woodland high above the hurrying river.

Dawdle along the lovely path, where bluebells pierce a carpet of bronzed leaves, and follow it as it drops down to a wide green pasture beside the river. Do not cross the footbridge, but continue over the turf to join a wide track continuing ahead. This climbs out of the trees onto Harden Road, where you turn right. Drop down the hill, again with care, to cross the wide arched Ireland Bridge, built in 1685 and widened in 1775, into Millgate. Turn left by the Old White Horse, once a coaching inn, and walk the quiet street to the parish church of All Saints, Bingley. Turn right just before the church into a short paved footpath to cross the A650. Continue along the walled footpath that leads to a tunnel under the railway. Stride on to reach the side of the canal, where you turn right. Pause here to see the three rise locks (22-24), built on the staircase principle, where the canal rises a spectacular 30ft. Stride beside the cut to pass between the mills of Bingley and continue on below more bridges (202-204). The towpath now takes you out into the countryside.

Pass below the Scourer Bridge (205), close to the Fisherman's Inn. Here snowdrops grow in profusion along the banks of the cut. Stride on past Dowley locks (20-21), where the canal has been raised 18ft 4in. Cross Dowley Gap Changeline Bridge (206), another attractive stone bridge where old men gather for a chat, to continue along the towpath, now on the opposite bank. Just beyond is the aqueduct seen earlier on the walk, where you take a gap stile at the start of the bridge. Walk the path that leads through the trees and follow it as it drops down to beside the river.

Stroll on along the quiet way to pass a spectacular weir just beyond the Bradford rowing club. Cross a small footbridge and continue ahead to take the third of three bridges over the river, this one for pedestrians only. Walk ahead to pass through a gap stile onto the towpath. Turn left to return to Saltaire and to rejoin your car.

Bridge 205

River Aire, Bingley

Walk 7: Circular walk from Bingley via Riddlesden

Distance:	6½ miles
Time:	3-4 hours
Maps:	OS Pathfinder 682 SE 03/13 Bradford (W Yorks) and 671 SE 04/14 Keighley and Ilkley
Terrain:	Easy walking all the way.

Park in the public car park behind Safeways supermarket at Bingley and walk downhill to the towpath. Turn left to walk past mills - including the Damart mill, with a huge chimney proclaiming its name - to continue by the three rise locks (22-24), where you joined the canal towpath on Walk 6.

Stroll on beside the quiet waterway to the foot of the famous Bingley five rise locks (25-29), which lift the canal 60ft up the Aire valley. On this spectacular staircase, the top gates of the bottom lock form the bottom gates of the lock above. Beside the top gates stands a cottage, the home of

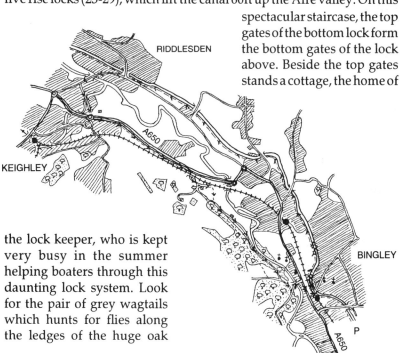

the lock keeper, who is kept very busy in the summer helping boaters through this daunting lock system. Look for the pair of grey wagtails which hunts for flies along the ledges of the huge oak

33

gates. A signpost close by tells you that you are now 16$^{1/4}$ miles from Leeds and 111 miles from Liverpool.

Continue on the towpath past many moored boats. The canal is now high above the Aire valley, with houses below to the left. A pair of swans comes close to the towpath, disturbing a dozen or more pairs of mallards and one smaller, rounder dabchick. Robins, wrens, chaffinches, crows and blackbirds move through the greening hawthorn bushes that line the way. Stride on along the towpath to cross Micklethwaite swing bridge (199) and then through Crossflatts. Just before Morton swing bridge (198A), look over the wall on the left to see the pretty Morton Beck hurrying through wooded banks, far below.

Now the canal curves gracefully past small farms where you can see sheep, cattle and donkeys. Greenfinches call from tall ash trees close to the water's edge. Pass under Swine Lane Bridge (198). Here a pair of goosanders idles among several mallards in the early spring sunshine. Suddenly the pair moves off, swimming with great speed, their heads well forward and their rounded backs just above the water.

Stride on until, on the far bank, you are level with the Marquis of Granby, a favoured hostelry with bargees of times gone by, on Hospital Road, a narrow lane. Pass Granby swing bridge (197A) and turn left to leave the towpath to walk down the short Granby Lane. Cross the A650 and walk into the delightful grounds of the National Trust-owned East Riddlesden Hall. You come to the side of a small lake first, the haunt of many ducks and gulls. Close by is a magnificent cruck barn. Beyond the lake stands the 17th-century hall, standing on a grassy mound overlooking the River Aire. The charming house is open to the public from April onwards.

Return to the A650 and turn left to walk the busy road, cross the River Aire and turn left just beyond the pelican crossing into Aireworth Road. Walk on to cross the River Worth and continue to the roundabout on the by-pass, which you cross. Away to the right are the chimneys of the textile town of Keighley. Once across the A-road walk forward in the direction of Worth village and then turn almost immediately into Airedale Road. Continue past the nursery school, the dairy, the tube works and the gasworks to join the footpath beside the by-pass which unfortunately has swallowed up the quiet way on the latest OS map.

Continue past the pig farm, it too divided by the highway, and then the well-screened sewage works on the left. To your right is the railway. Look for the hand gate on your right, which gives access to a track under the railway line. Beyond, turn left through a kissing gate to continue your walk, blissfully free of traffic. The footpath, lined with brambles that might cause problems in the summer, is fenced on both sides, with the railway embankment to your left. To the right stands Marley Hall, a charming farmhouse with wooded slopes behind. Suddenly the walk along the by-pass seems well worthwhile.

Beyond the fenced path, bear diagonally right along a clear path to join a track. To your right foxglove leaves green the floor of the steeply sloping mixed woodland. Continue past Cophurst Farm to walk along a walled and hedged lane that leads to Raven Royd, where there has been a farm since the 12th century. Cross the stream that runs through the cobbled yard and then continue on past the pleasing old dwelling.

Look left over the wall of the track to catch your first glimpse of the River Aire. It flows far below, with wooded slopes on its far bank. At the junction of paths, take the left branch, which is tree-lined on both sides, to drop down to the side of the stately river. Walk on to pass All Saints Church on the far bank and then the Damart chimney comes into view. Pass the glorious weir, where the water descends in a flurry of white-topped foam, to the gap stile onto the B6429.

Turn left to cross Ireland Bridge. Turn left again beyond the Old White Horse Inn and take the footpath right just before the church. Cross the A650 and continue along the walled footpath to pass under the railway. Stride on through the allotments to the canal where you turn right to return to the car park.

Five-rise locks, Bingley

35

The Cruck Barn, Riddlesden Hall

Walk 8: Circular walk from Riddlesden

Distance:	5¹/₂ miles
Time:	2-3 hours
Map:	OS Pathfinder 671 SE 04/14 Keighley and Ilkley
Terrain:	Easy walking

Park close to East Riddlesden Hall, where if you did not manage a visit on Walk 7 you might be tempted to do so on this one. The 17th-century manor house built in stone with its magnificent cruck barn is owned by the National Trust. It is open to the public from April onwards. Watch the many ducks on the lake - feeding them is a great attraction for the very young of Riddlesden. Sit in the small delectable walled garden at the front of the house and enjoy the lovingly tended plants.

Leave the hall, cross the A650 and climb the slope to the towpath, just west of Granby swing bridge (197A). Turn left to begin the pleasing walk beside the tranquil waterway. Continue past a stone warehouse, with a canopy projecting over the water, to pass the Stockbridge swing bridge (197). Pussy willow in full blossom lines the bank and a wren scolds from the grass on the far side of the cut.

Head on past Leache's swing bridge (196) and out into the early spring country- side where

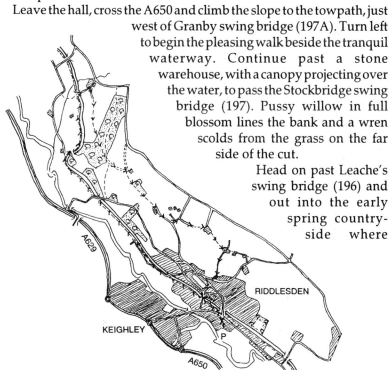

37

Two herons

coltsfoot, celandines and dog's mercury flower. Look left to see the brownstone buildings of Elam Grange. Tall beeches still with pointed buds tightly wrapped, now line the opposite bank and to the left stretches the extensive Keighley golf course.

Beyond Booth's swing bridge (195) rhododendrons line the far bank, trailing green leaves in the water. Promise yourself a visit to see this lovely gracious stretch of the canal when the bushes are laden with flowers. Enjoy the scene at Low Holden, where colourful boats tie up beneath more tall beech. Then pass under the white-railed high level Lodge Hill Bridge (194) that elegantly spans the waterway. From Alder Carr Wood come the restless calls of a pair of jays.

At Holden swing bridge (193), cross the canal and walk up the walled track towards Howden Park Farm. Pass through two gates and turn right to continue along the walled way, which can be muddy after rain. From the pastures comes the bleating of many lambs and ewes. Beyond the gate continue ahead, with a wall to your left, into a pasture from where a pair of herons flies off after feeding. At the next gate, beneath a pylon which strides a drystone wall, bear diagonally left over a pasture, following the line of the overhead power lines, to a stile into Alder Carr Wood.

Stand on the stile and look down on the graciously meandering canal, the wintry sun changing it to a ribbon of silver. Continue right through the deciduous woodland, with a wall to your right, and follow the path as it climbs steeply up the slope in the same direction as the ubiquitous power lines. From the branches of the beech trees come the calls of blue, great and long tailed tits. Honeysuckle in full leaf clings to any branch it can.

The path through the wood leads to a gap stile in the boundary wall. Beyond, walk ahead to a large ladder stile - again stand on the top for a magnificent view, this time of Airedale. Stride slightly right across the

38

next field to another tall ladder stile to the right of Jaytail Farm. From now on the high-level path passes through bracken, skirting the golf course and keeping parallel with a wall on the left.

Straddle the stile in the boundary fence and step across Clough Beck. Climb the slope ahead to pass through a gate and walk to the access track to Wood Head Lodge. Stroll on along the upper track, keeping to the left of High Wood Head. Press on along the walled way to Banks Lane, where you turn left. Here Jacob sheep have several tiny black and white lambs.

Turn right into a reinforced lane, with a sign for Larkfield Old Barn. A flock of mistle thrushes restlessly moves through the sycamores lining the way. Carry on until you reach a white metal gate beside a farm gate. Pass through and head on to a stile in a fence. Beyond, stride on to pass through a farm gate to The Height. Turn right and follow the muddy track as it swings right and then left. Pass through another gate and follow the cart track across the pastures to the next farm. By the deserted buildings, turn right and begin the pleasing descent to Riddlesden, walking beside a small stream shadowed by trees.

Pass through a gate where daffodils and snowdrops flower and walk on to the Ilkley Road. Turn right to take the signposted cobbled footpath on your left that drops downhill, opposite the Willow Tree public house. Cross Banks Lane to continue down the signposted steep steps and cobbled way to Scott Lane, where you turn left. After 20yds turn right to cross the swing bridge (197) to regain the towpath. Turn left to walk beside the waterway to Granby swing bridge. leave the canal here to rejoin your car.

White-railed footbridge -
Alder Carr Wood behind   39

Silsden

Walk 9 Circular walk from Silsden

Distance:	8 miles
Time:	4-5 hours
Map:	OS Pathfinder 671 SE 04/14 Keighley and Ilkley
Terrain:	Easy walking all the way. Farm tracks muddy after rain. On this lovely walk it is wise to use your map, and much more fun to work out for yourself the position of the stiles.

Park in the free car park in the centre of the pleasing brownstone town of Silsden. Notice the splendid churches of Our Lady of Mount Carmel and St James, which face each other. Walk south along the main street, which is lined with attractive shops, and pass the impressive Methodist church with its colourful garden. Continue to the Silsden Bridge (191A) which you cross to drop down on the left to the towpath.

Walk south-east to pass a low stone building, once stables for the horses that pulled the barges, and which today is still used as a stable. Carry on past Brunthwaite swing bridge (192) and pass through the stone stile on your right. From here you can see the two sturdy well preserved lime-kilns, once used to process the lime-stone that came by canal from the north-west.

Rejoin the tow-path and head on to Holden swing bridge (193), which you cross. Walk ahead to pass through the attrac-tive Howden Park Farm to Holden Lane, where you turn left. Continue along the lane, with

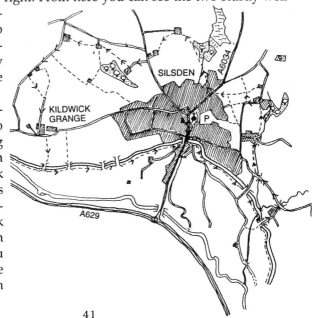

the golf course to your right, to take the signposted footpath on your right, just before Brunthwaite Beck. At the next gate, cross the stone slab footbridge and continue by the footbridge on the signposted way to Lightbank Lane at Brunthwaite.

Turn left and then right to continue beside the lively beck. Enjoy this quiet patch of green, from where you can hear the excited courting curlews in the fields round about. Look for a pair of grey wagtails prospecting for a nest site. Celandines spangle the bank to the hurrying water and fat buds show bright green in the early spring sunshine.

Climb the signposted steps and ascend the stiled pastures to Swartha, where you turn left. Where Swartha Lane swings left, pass through a stone stile, turn right to pass through another and continue to the hedge. Do not pass through but turn left to drop downhill through a pasture and allotments to Bolton Road.

Cross the road and turn left. Take the next right turn and walk in front of Longbottom Green Garage to pass in front of the lovely old cottages at Town Head (1696). Cross the road and walk behind the houses on the right, ascending Browcliffe. Follow the lane where it swings left and walk ahead to descend a lovely tree-lined footpath into delightful countryside. Climb the stile and follow the footpath right as it descends to cross a footbridge over Silsden Beck.

Straddle two stiles and climb uphill, keeping the wood to your right. At the top left corner of the trees, look for the stile in a short stone wall on your right and look behind you to enjoy a magnificent view over the glorious Yorkshire countryside and of Silsden with its mill chimneys and church spires. Beyond, walk close beside the hedge on your left towards Hay Hills Farm. From this path you can see, north-east, Silsden Reservoir, a lovely patch of blue, much frequented by black-headed gulls. Fifty yards before a silage pit cross a plank footbridge over a ditch on the left to a broken fence, which you climb. Carry on over the pasture

Grey wagtails

42

Footbridge over
Silsden Beck

to a waymarked
stone stile in the
right corner, close
by the farm fence.
Climb it to reach a
cart track, where
you turn right.
Stride on to
take a faintly way-
marked gate on the left, just before the end of the track. Beyond, follow
the telegraph poles across the pasture to a stile. Continue ahead beside
the hedge on the right, and continue to Raikes Head Farm. Walk
between the farm buildings and then past a charming barn and some
beautiful cottages on the right, to Bradley Road, where you turn left.

Take the signposted farm track on the right. Just before Low Bracken
Hill Farm, turn right to walk beside a ditch on your left to a gap stile to
the right of a gate. Bear slightly right across a huge field to a waymarked
stile and a plank footbridge over a tiny beck. Walk to a gate in the far left
corner of the wall, passing Hole Farm on your right. Beyond, turn right
and walk 30yds to a stile on your right, which you cross. Walk on, with
the hedge to your left. To continue ahead to Bridge House Farm, either
climb through a hole in the wall on your left or pass through a gate on
your right in the wall ahead and then return to the track to the farm.

Stroll on to New Lane and turn left. Walk the narrow lane through
the high pastures, where green plovers perform their acrobatic aerial
courtship. Pass Great Slack to take a gap stile just before the few ruins
of Little Slack. Cross the pasture to the step stile in the wall and bear left
to a stile a short way along the boundary wall on your left. Walk to the
far left corner and beyond the stile in the wall look for the next one, a gap
stile opposite, left, which gives access to a pleasing walled track, the
haunt of meadow pipits.

Continue on the reinforced track to pass Kildwick Grange on your
right. Turn left and then right to take a signposted grassy way that drops
down through the pastures to cross Grange swing bridge (188). Turn
left to begin the pleasing saunter along the towpath to Silsden, passing
three more swing bridges - Lanehouse (189), Woodside (190) and
Cowling (191) - on the way. This stretch of the cut curves gracefully and
is lined with trees and edged with pastures.

43

Church of St Andrew, Kildwick in Craven - the 'Lang Kirk'

Walk 10: Circular walk from Kildwick

Distance:	6½ miles
Time:	3-4 hours
Maps:	OS Pathfinder 671 SE 04/14 Keighley and Ilkley
	670 SD 84/94 Barnoldswick and Earby
Terrain:	Easy walking

N ewby Road comes close beside the canal at Kildwick and at this point there is a small public car park. Approaching by car from the south, you pass below a narrow skewed aqueduct carrying the waterway.

Walk east along the narrow road, past the charming stone houses and the lower end of steep narrow streets, quaintly named Back Mary Street and Mary Street, which spill down to the water's edge. Continue to Parsons Bridge (186), which you cross to visit the church of St Andrew, mentioned in the Domesday Book. St Andrew's is often described as the Lang Kirk because

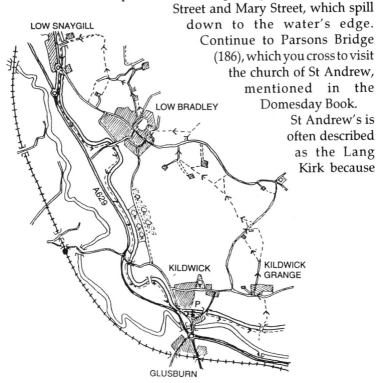

45

of its great length - 150ft. Look for the fine weather-vane on the tower, the large cheery clock that overlooks the churchyard and the splendid sundial above the vestry door. A helpful verger will unlock the door if you wish to see inside the church. Notice particularly its beautifully carved choir pews and the 14th-century effigy of Sir Robert de Stiverton, Lord of the Manor of Steeton.

Return to the towpath, pass under bridge 186 and stride eastwards past Warehouse swing bridge (187). Here the way is lined with blackthorn - a cloud of blossom - and hawthorn in soft green leaf. Beneath the bushes flower celandines, white dead nettle, ground ivy, butterbur, cow parsley and bluebells. Greenfinches, chaffinches and pied wagtails flit through the branches and settle on the walls along the path.

Next you come to Grange swing bridge (188), reached on the last walk, which you cross. Walk ahead up the slope through a rather wet gill, from where you are serenaded by courting curlews. Continue to the waymarked gate to the road and turn left to pass several attractive dwellings. Just before Kildwick Grange turn right into the signposted footpath to pass Grange Farm, which once belonged to the canons of Bolton.

Climb up beside the beck, which is now lined with primroses, golden saxifrage and wood sorrel. Pass through the gate to continue along the grassy walled way. Look for the stile in the wall on your left and, beyond, walk the few steps to another on your right. Follow the wall on your left to a stepped stile at a junction of walls. Strike half right to a stile over a very small stretch of wall. Continue on the same right diagonal to another stepped stile and then walk ahead to pass the ruined Little Slack on your left to the road, where you turn right.

Pass Great Slack and take the stile leading from a triangular patch of ground on your left. Stride beside the wall on your right, passing a copse of beech to another ladder stile. Walk across the pasture, bearing slightly left to the next stile. Look left to see Kildwick Moor stretching away into the distance. Skylarks rise on quivering wing until mere specks in the sky. Continue to the right of a sycamore and beech copse to a gap stile. Beyond, walk ahead to a step stile in the far left corner, through a pasture full of sheep and lambs.

Once over the stile continue in the same direction, with the wall on your right. Take care over the next stile, which is damaged, and then continue on the downward sloping stiled way, still beside the wall. From here you have your first glimpse of a gracious curve on the canal and of the hills beyond Skipton. Pass through the stile to the left of a gate

Stone stile (don't cross this one)

onto a good reinforced track, access to Lower Sire Bank Farm, where you turn right to walk to Jackson's Lane.

Turn right and take the stepped stile over the wall on your left. Cut across the corner of the field on a right diagonal to a stile and, beyond, walk to the end of a very short wall. Turn left and continue down the slope to a gate. (Ignore the superb stile to the left of the gate.) Climb the blocked gate and walk beside the wall on your left towards Low Bradley, which is snugly tucked into a hollow in the gentle hills. Pass through the gate in the bottom left corner and then take the stile immediately on your right into a walled cart track. Walk the track into Low Bradley and follow it right to pass the pleasing Old Hall. Look for the plaque with 1678 and the initials IBD on it.

Stroll beside the house and take the easy-to-miss narrow tree-lined footpath ahead to a gated stile. Continue on a left diagonal to come beside a pretty stream and then a stile to the access track to Ghyll Farm. Turn left and then right to pass through a gate to the left of a derelict cornmill. The footpath continues up steps to a gap stile and then below a hedgerow on the left. Two more stiles bring you to a road where you turn right. Climb the steep flower-lined lane to a welcome bench seat. Sit here and enjoy the view down to the village and to the outlying slopes criss-crossed with walls.

Climb the stile behind the seat and continue, with the wall to your left, to a gap stile. Stride on in the same direction to the next gap stile and then onto a stepped stile into a grassy walled track, which you cross to take the stile opposite. Continue ahead over three easy-to-see stiles. Look for the next one in the wall on your left and then stride ahead in the same direction towards Gill Bottom. Here take the small gated stile hidden in the gill near to the right corner of the pasture. Cross the beck and walk left up the slope to pass the farmhouse on your right. Continue down the access track to cross Bradley swing bridge (182A) over the canal. Turn left and continue under Bradley Bridge (182).

Walk past the premises of Snaygill narrow boat hire business with its many colourful boats tied up along the canal. From now directions are not needed. The way takes you beside the placid water, where the path is lined with spring flowers. Bushes and trees are alive with small birds, serenading the sun and hoping to impress a mate. Woods carpeted with bluebells slope down to the water's edge. Moorhens run over the banking and then hurry across the water when disturbed.

Look left high on the hill, to see Lower Sire Bank Farm, where you walked earlier. Then the canal curves away from the noisy Keighley Road to the quieter Low Bradley. Dawdle along the gracefully curving waterway, which is overlooked by Low Bradley Moor and Farnhill Moor, with its Jubilee Tower. A heron flies just above the water and then rises with legs straggling over the trees on the opposite bank. Pass Farnhill Wood and then Farnhill Hall and into Farnhill and on past Milking Hill swing bridge (184) and on to Kildwick.

Before you leave this lovely corner of Yorkshire, walk to bridge 186 once again and turn left to climb the hedged paved trod to a road. Turn right to see Kildwick Hall (1673), a magnificent house now owned by

the Morrison supermarket family. It was once the home of the Currers. Charlotte Brontë's *nom de plume* was Currer Bell and it is believed she took the name from this family. The wrought iron gates support a pair of lions which, so the legend goes, walk down to the canal after dark for a drink. Return to your car by descending one of the steep streets that drop down to the canal side.

Primroses, wood sorrel and golden saxifrage

48

Walk 11: Circular walk from Springs Branch

Distance:	2¹/₂ miles
Time:	1-2 hours
Map:	OS Outdoor Leisure 10 Yorkshire Dales southern area or
	OS Pathfinder 661 SD 85/95 Skipton & Hellifield
Terrain:	Easy walking but paths in the wood can be muddy.

This walk takes you along the Springs Branch of the Leeds and Liverpool Canal. It is 770yds long and passes through the town of Skipton, hidden in a steep-sided ravine. Skipton Castle towers overhead and the Earl of Thanet, an 18th-century occupant, had the branch constructed to carry limestone from his quarries upstream.

Park in the Coach Street extension car park close to the Springs Branch. Cross the road and Belmont Bridge (178) to join a footpath that runs between the waterway and the hurrying Eller Beck. Here colourful boats are tied and enthusiasts busily refurbish them. Pass under another bridge and begin the glorious walk to Skipton Woods. This path is lined with alders and the beck on your left dances merrily on its way.

Soon the path, deep in its gill, passes beneath the forbidding walls of the 900-year-old castle. Lady Anne Clifford, the 17th-century landowner, was born in it and she restored it, late in her life, to its former

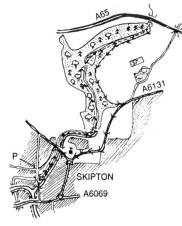

glory. Continue past several rushing falls and then cross the beck by a footbridge. Turn right to walk through a large gate and carry on past the Old Sawmill to a gate into Skipton Woods. The woods are cared for by the Woodland Trust who invite visitors.

Stroll ahead through sycamore and beech trees beneath which flower bluebells and wild garlic, and where birdsong fills the air. Look upstream to some more white-topped falls and then take the footbridge across the lively beck. Beyond is a seat beside a

49

Skipton Castle from Springs Branch

Skipton, Springs Branch

large pond edged with clumps of golden kingcups, where a mallard marshals her ducklings. Strike left from here to return to the side of the beck for a dramatic view of the foaming falls below a weir. Return to the path and walk on, where wrens and willow warblers proclaim their territories. Here you might see a kingfisher. A sparrow hawk flies silently among the trees, a brown short-winged, long-tailed predator hungry for its next meal.

The path, muddy in places, keeps beside the now placid beck until you almost reach the by-pass (A65). At the end of the way turn right and climb the steepish path to the top of the slope to join a delightful path which returns downstream but keeps high above the beck. Here in small clearings orange-tipped butterflies flit about the lush vegetation. Follow the path as it bears left to cross an old bridge and then continue high above the pond seen earlier. Stroll on, with a steep tree-lined slope to the right. It is carpeted with bluebells and wood anemones.

Pause in a small clearing, high above the beck - noisy now that you have passed the weir - to sit in a charming seat hewn out of the base of a huge felled tree. Dawdle along the way, keeping beside a wall, and then bear left to head on along a walled track, with pastures to the left and, beyond, the crags of Embsay. From Embsay quarries came much of the limestone transported along Springs Branch.

Swing right to walk to a road called The Bailey. Turn right and descend, passing the huge edifice of Skipton Building Society on your

Redwings eating hawthorn berries

left. A short distance on, sheep and lambs graze in a pasture enclose by a crenellated wall.

Pass the main entrance to the castle, the only part of the original Norman structure to be seen. Walk on in front of Holy Trinity Church, also extensively restored by Lady Anne, and follow the road right to return to the side of the Springs Branch and the car park.

Mallard with ducklings in the kingcups

Walk 12: Linear walk from Skipton

Distance:	2 miles to Thorlby swing bridge (174)
	³/₄ mile to Snaygill swing bridge (181)
Time:	2 hours
	³/₄ hour
Maps:	OS Pathfinder 670 SD 84/94 Barnoldswick & Earby
	661 SD 85/95 Skipton & Hellifield
	Landranger 103 Blackburn, Burnley
	Outdoor Leisure 10 Yorkshire Dales southern area
Terrain:	Easy walking all the way.

P ark in the Cavendish Road car park beside the canal in the centre of the attractive stone-built town of Skipton, sometimes called "The Gateway to the Dales". Join the towpath and walk left where a signpost tells you that you are 98 miles from Liverpool. Continue under Belmont Bridge (178), and then look right for a pleasing view of the hump- 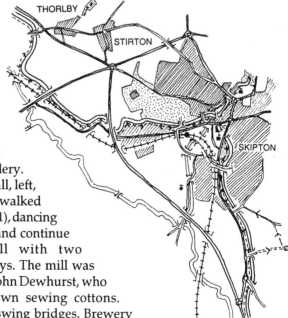 backed bridge over the Springs Branch where it joins the cut (see walk 11). Colourful flowers and picturesque boats edge the placid waterway. Here boats may be hired and there is a chandlery.

Look over the wall, left, to see Eller Beck (walked beside also on walk 11), dancing over its rocky bed, and continue past a huge mill with two magnificent chimneys. The mill was opened in 1870 for John Dewhurst, who produced well-known sewing cottons. Stride on past two swing bridges, Brewery (177) and Gawflat (176), and many moored

53

Skipton - the beginning of the Springs Branch

boats. Scattered trees grow along the far bank and in places pastures run down to the water's edge.

And then the canal becomes tree-lined on both sides. Here dog rose and elder are in blossom and below flower woody cranesbill and meadow sweet. Look over the pastures on the right to Skipton's auction mart, reminding you that sheep thrive on the surrounding pastures as they did long ago when the Anglo-Saxons named the town Scip-tun, meaning sheep town.

Where the canal moves into the open countryside and curves right, red clover, angelica and hop trefoil grow along its banks. Pass under the modern, elegant road bridge that carries the A629 and, beyond, look for the milestone that announces you are now $30^{1/4}$ miles from Leeds. Stroll on, past fishermen, out into pastoral glory and follow the gracefully curving cut. Head on past Niffany swing bridge (175) and leave the towpath to continue along the roadside. After 100yds you rejoin the towpath, which is lined with dog daisies.

Look left through trees to see the railway and a road - all three forms of transport within 50yds of each other. Families of mallards and moorhens come to the bank, hoping to be fed. Pass below the bridge, over which runs the A59. Look for the house martins nesting tight up against the arch of the bridge, the birds apparently unperturbed by the noise and the frequent vibrations. Beyond, you can see the glorious green slopes of Flasby Fell.

Follow the towpath as the canal curves gently below Hoober Hill. Swallows dive over the water after flies, and curlew call

Dewhurst's Mill, Skipton

from the pastures where they stand guard over their brood. Pause on your walk to watch the myriad of minnows swimming as one, just below the surface. Look also for shoals of larger fish that dart back and forth in the sun-warmed water.

And then the River Aire, which rises to Malhamdale, comes into view on your left. Here, in contrast to its mature waters walked beside in earlier walks, it is narrow and silvery. Then the canal curves left. Here you might be passed by a Skipton and Craven blue barge that glides slowly and peacefully along the waterway. This is a specially adapted boat for people with disabilities. The next bridge is Thorlby swing (174). Here again house martins nest below the structure, unperturbed by the frequent trip across the water.

This is the point of return, back along the canal to Skipton. Or you may wish to use a Pennine bus, Gargrave to Skipton, which travels along the A65. This A road runs parallel to the canal and is reached by crossing the swing bridge (174).

On reaching the town you might wish to continue along the towpath. Walk to Snaygill swing bridge (181) (where you returned south on walk 10) just beyond Randell's Hotel on the right. This small extension of the walk ensures you walk the whole of the towpath - from Leeds to Liverpool!

Cross the bridge and continue ahead to pass through Snaygill Farm.

Walk on along the farm track to just before Gill Bottom. Here strike left across the pasture to step across a narrow stream and onto a footbridge over a second. Continue ahead to the narrow road in front of Horse Close Farm. Follow the way left and continue along it to rejoin the towpath to stroll back, north, to the car park.

Wild roses and elder

56

Walk 13: Circular walk from Gargrave

Distance:	9 miles
Time:	4-4¹/₂ hours
Map:	OS Pathfinder 661 SD 85/95 Skipton & Hellifield
Terrain:	Easy walking for most of the route. A short steep climb to Sharp Haw.

Park in the free car park in West Street, Gargrave, which lies to the north of High Street. Stride Chew Lane to the canal towpath at Higherland Bridge (170). Turn right, continue past Eshton Road lock (31) and Eshton Road Bridge (171). Pass under Ray Bridge (172) and walk out into the lovely gentle pastures of Yorkshire. Cross an aqueduct. Close by, men and boys fish for perch, roach, bream and pike. Meadow pipits rise, carolling into the warm summer air. Carry on past Highgate swing bridge (173) to Thorlby swing bridge (174), which you cross. Head on along a cart track. Cross the A65 to stroll a glorious country lane that passes through the village of Thorlby and onto the cross-roads at Stirton. Turn left

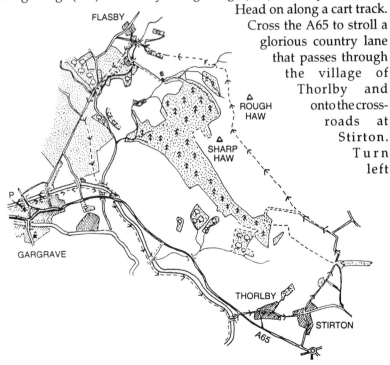

57

Gargrave, looking towards Flasby Fell

Grey squirrel in beech tree

and walk a narrower lane below beeches, where a grey squirrel ascends grey bark. Overhead a pair of kestrels utter their eerie call as they hover in search of prey.

After nearly a mile take the second footpath on the left, signposted Bridleway to Flasby. This gated, waymarked track leads out onto the rolling moorland of Skyrakes. Look for the path leading right from the track - the right of way passing between Rough Haw (1400ft) and Sharp Haw. Here divert and walk ahead to take the ladder stile that gives access to Sharp Haw triangulation point and a breathtaking view. You can see Embsay Crag, Crookrise Crag, Cracoe church, Grassington, Malham Cove, Clitheroe, the great whaleback of Pendle, Skipton and beyond. The enclosure nearby is an Iron Age hill-top site.

Strike right (east) off the summit and pass through a gap in the wall below. Walk ahead through heather to a gate, where some boulder-hopping might be necessary. Carry on below the boulder-strewn skirt of Rough Haw to take a path, right, through bracken, waymarked by a blue capped post. Follow the path as it comes close to a wall on your right and then descends the lovely slope, zigzagging to a gate, halfway along the wall ahead. Beyond, go to a gate in the far left corner to walk a walled reinforced track, which is edged with hawthorns, to descend into Flasby.

Embsay Moor from Flasby Fell

Cross Flasby Beck and walk ahead to turn left into a track opposite Flasby Grange Hall and just before the postbox in a wall. Walk to a lane to a signpost that stands in a pasture on the left and take the gate on the right. Cut left across the corner of the field to a stile. Walk ahead for 20yds and pass through the right of two gates. Continue, passing the splendid Flasby Hall on your left. Join its access track for 40yds and then strike right to the edge of a conifer plantation to walk a track, covered with chippings, to a kissing gate to the road.

Turn left and walk downhill to cross Eshton Bridge. On the right stands the stately Eshton Hall built around 1826. At the T-junction, take the footpath on your left, signposted Holme Bridge. Continue left to pass through three stiles (the first not waymarked and not on the OS map) and onto a fourth in the corner beside a larch plantation. Go downhill over two stiles to a stiled path, left, over the aqueduct on the canal. Cross the footbridge ahead and then another over the placid waterway. Turn right and dawdle beside the lovely cut to return to Gargrave.

Walk 14: Circular walk south from Gargrave

Distance:	7¹⁄₂ miles
Time:	3-4 hours
Map:	OS Landranger 103 Blackburn, Burnley and surrounding area
	OS Pathfinder 661 SD 85/95 Skipton & Hellifield
Terrain:	Easy walking all the way.

Gargrave, with its picturesque cottages and tea shops, lies on the edge of the National Park. Generally the River Aire, flowing alongside its main street (A65), dances and chuckles but when in spate it rages, pushing the many ducks into quieter backwaters. Park in the free car park in West Street, which lies north of the main street (as for walk 13). Cross the A65 and the bridge over the Aire to continue along Church Street, where you might like to visit 16th-century St Andrew's. Just beyond, take the Pennine Way, sign-posted on the right. Follow the well-marked track and then the path out of the village. Look for a weasel (reddy brown fur and no black tip to its tail) hunting along the bank of a stream. Climb the gentle pastures to join a tree-lined narrow track where you turn left to cross the railway. Beyond, dawdle on to a seat well placed to enable you to enjoy a spectacular view across the village to Flasby Fell. Once over the cattle-grid, bear off left, leaving the track, and stride on towards a tall post on Scaleber Hill.

The Double Bridge, East Marton

cri\
Weasel

Continue over the waymarked stiles, deep in the glorious countryside, to turn right as directed. Stroll on with a silver birch copse and a narrow stream to your right to take the waymarked footbridge over the beck to an arrowed stile. Ascend the slope ahead to straddle the stile to a track where you turn left.

Look for the next stile, which you climb, in the wall on your left. Beyond, walk a green swathe to take a stile into a delightful walled track. Follow the waymarks out of the track and across a meadow with pleasant views, left, across rolling pastures. Continue to a stile onto a narrow lane, where you turn left, which passes through woodland to Williamson Bridge (162) over the canal. Do not cross but join the towpath to walk to Double Arched Bridge (161). The lower one was once used by packhorses and the upper one, built when the road was raised, now carries the A59, Skipton to Gisburn.

Follow the towpath, under the twin bridges, and walk on to cross Church Bridge (160). A delectable footpath continues to the church of St Peter, Marton, which has a battlemented Norman tower. Within, see a fragment of a Saxon cross, intricately carved, and a Norman font. Return to the towpath and walk back to Williamson Bridge. Here you might like to make a diversion into the small hamlet, where there is a public house and a restaurant, before you continue along the towpath.

From now on the walk back to Gargrave is all pleasure. The towpath passes through trees which cling to the sides of a short cutting made by those 18th-century engineers as they took the canal over the backbone of the Pennines. Pass Langber Bridge (163). Then the canal winds back and forth, following the contours. On the towpath you cover a mile or

Sparrowhawk

more just to progress less than half. Pass Newton Bridge (164). Walk the narrow road when the towpath ceases, cross Newton Changeline Bridge (165), take the stile on the left and pass under the bridge. Look for the white vertical stripe on the bridge, placed there to help night-time navigation. Continue on the towpath, now on the opposite bank.

Stroll past the superb flight of six locks (36-41) at Bank Newton, which lower the water level 56ft 0^{1}/$_{2}$in, as you begin the descent towards the Aire gap. Here you might see the petrol-blue flash of a kingfisher. Look also for the white triangular mileposts, with smaller ones indicating the quarter miles. Then comes a little more road walking, where boatmen had to walk with their horses. Beyond the road bridge, drop down to the towpath and pass under Priestholme Changeline Bridge (168), to continue on the opposite bank. Carry on to cross Priest Holme aqueduct, which takes you over the River Aire, and beyond continue past the Gargrave locks (33-35) which lower the canal by 28ft 3in. Pass below the A65 and head on to Higherland Bridge (170) at Chew Lane. Leave the towpath and walk right into Gargrave to your car.

Milestone

Walk 15: Circular walk from Thornton-in-Craven

Distance:	7¹/₂ miles
Time:	4 hours
Map:	OS Pathfinder 670 SD 84/94 Barnoldswick & Earby
	661 SD 85/95 Skipton & Hellifield
Terrain:	Easy walking all the way

Park on a very large layby on Church Road (B6252), close to the little church of St Mary's at Thornton-in Craven. The present sturdy stone building with its solid square tower, set on high ground above the village, is 15th century. Go inside and enjoy the peace of the lovely church with its splendid 17th-century oak pews. Early in the year snowdrops flower among the graves and to the west of the church is a spring, covered with a domed structure placed there in the 18th century.

Continue uphill into the village, passing almshouses "provided for five poor women" as you go. At the T-junction, turn left to walk the main street (A56), which is lined with attractive stone houses. Continue past the stocks on the small green and then the post office. Turn left beyond Rock House into Cam Lane to join the Pennine Way, and stride uphill to pass the school. Ignore the first footpath and walk on along the

Thornton-in-Craven
- cottages

Greenberfield

pleasing lane and then the continuing cart track. From here there are extensive views across the rolling pastures to Flasby Fell, where Sharp Haw and Rough Haw spike the sky.

Carry on past Old Cote Farm and stroll on to leave the farm track, taking a signposted gate on the right. Beyond, follow the Pennine Way sign directing you diagonally left over the pasture. Drop down the slope to cross Carr Beck on a plank bridge. Pass through the next two stiles and then, maintaining the same general direction, climb uphill where a well-placed arrow on a stone keeps you on the path. The next waymark is found on a telegraph pole. Then stroll downhill, with a good view of the picturesque East Marton church, visited on the last walk. Continue to a stile that gives access to the towpath, where you turn left.

Walk the tight bends of the lovely contouring cut, where the hedges lining the path are alive with small birds. Soon the church at Thornton comes into view across the gentle undulating pastures. Just before and after passing under South Field bridge (159), look for several derelict loading bays, where coal was removed from boats and stored. Here two pairs of goosanders fish the dark waters and then fly off quickly, circling overhead before settling further along the canal.

Look left to see the first of the two Rolls-Royce factories in this area. Beyond you can see the pretty 16th-century church of St Mary's-le-Ghyll surrounded by trees. It has a three-decker pulpit, box pews and

Pair of goosanders

a 14th-century font. Continue along the towpath to cross the county border, leaving Yorkshire and entering Lancashire.

Pass over Greenberfield Changeline Bridge (158), now walking part of the Pendle Way, to continue past the Greenberfield locks (42-44), a series of three which raise the water 29ft 1in. Originally the locks formed a staircase, opening directly from one to the next, a method which made heavy demands on the water supply. Following several canal closures because of water shortages, changes had to be made. A diversion of the canal enabled the locks to be spread out. Even so water was often scarce and six reservoirs were constructed to fill the summit pond. The last to be built was Winterburn at Gargrave and a 9-mile pipeline carries the water to the outlet just above the lock keeper's cottage, which stands beside the second lock.

You are now walking at 487ft above sea level and the highest point of the Leeds and Liverpool Canal. Continue past the cottage and look for the small square building over the pipeline outlet, dated 1893. Beyond are convenient seats for picnics. Pass under Greenberfield Bridge (156) and walk on by many colourful boats moored for the winter. Here a milepost tells you that you are 41$^{1/}$₄miles from Leeds and 86 from Liverpool. Then you reach Barnoldswick and can see its many chimneys, with the great bulk of Pendle Hill slumbering behind.

Continue under Coate's Bridge (154A) and then on to pass the second Rolls-Royce factory, once a cotton mill. It is good to see that the stepped roof has been retained - stepped to allow the entry of northern light for the weavers. Once the town had 17 cotton mills but now it has only one.

Just before Long Ing Bridge (153), pass through the gate to the right and cross the bridge to join the towpath, now on the opposite bank. Stride on past another factory and then move out into the pleasant countryside once more. On the far bank is Lower Park Marina, where boats are built under a huge polythene "tent". Pass under Cockshott Bridge (152) and then walk by a solitary stone abutment, all that remains of a bridge that carried a now-dismantled railway.

Walk beneath the next road bridge, Park Bridge (151A), and continue past another mooring where an angler fishes for roach. You have now reached Salterforth. Here just before the Anchor Inn, close to Salterforth Bridge (151), leave the towpath by a small parking area on the left to walk left along Salterforth Lane. Cross Kelbrook Road and continue ahead. Head up Cross Lane, climbing Chapel Hill. Follow the lane as it swings right and ignore the first footpath. Cross the bridge over the dismantled railway. Continue up the narrow tree-lined lane into the quiet countryside. Walk the sharp right bend in the lane and, where it swings left, take the signposted footpath on the right to pass Bawmier Farm on the left of the outbuildings, following the waymarks.

Carry on over the field to the next gap stile and then to another on your left to continue in the same direction. Climb the next stile. To your right lies Earby and away to the left you can see St Mary's-le-Ghyll. The next stile lies ahead, a third of the way along the fence. Stride on to a stone stile, with a derelict barn to the left. Walk ahead to the boundary fence and here be sure to take the left of two stiles into a pasture where power lines cross. Continue in the same general direction, north-east, with one power line to your right and the other to your left.

Cross the large pasture to pass through a gap with a hedge to your left and a ditch to your right. Continue in the same direction to a stile to the left of a large hedgerow ash where you step across another small stream. Go on, bearing right from the stile, with the stream to your right.

When the stream veers away right walk ahead to a stile to the left of a gate. Beyond, head on to a signposted gate, which gives access to the Earby Road. Do not join it, but strike up the pasture, moving away from the road to a stile in the top left corner. Cross right over the corner of the next pasture to a kissing gate. Beyond stride across the pasture to a stile to the road, opposite the church, where you have parked.

Snowdrops and ivy

69

Foulridge Lower Reservoir ('Lake Burwain') with Pendle Hill and Blacks Tower in the background

Walk 16: Circular walk from Foulridge Canal Wharf

Distance:	6¹/₂ miles
Time:	3-4 hours
Map:	OS Pathfinder 670 SD 84/94 Barnoldswick & Earby
Terrain:	Easy walking. The track on White Moor can be very wet.

British Waterways' car park at Foulridge Canal Wharf lies next to the canal beyond the buildings of the wharf. Many ducks crowd the water and sit on the ice when the cut is frozen. Walk back beside the buildings to see the entrance to the Foulridge tunnel, which was constructed between 1790 and 1796. It took five years to build and cost many lives; some victims were buried in the canal bank. The tunnel has no towpath so tow horses were walked along the surface above. Until 1880 boats were "legged through" and then steam tugs - with engines at both ends so that they did not need to be turned round - pulled the boats through.

Around this eastern end of the 1640yd-long tunnel lies the quiet village of Foulridge, set in a valley with Noyna Hill to the east and Pasture Head to the west. It was a community of farmers and handloom weavers until the construction of the canal brought navvies into the

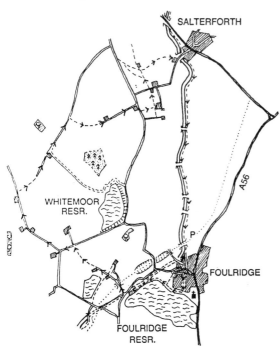

71

Foulridge

community. Enjoy the tea rooms in the old wharf office and stables before you start, or at the end of your walk. You can enjoy a cruise by boat through a tunnel or along the attractive summit level.

Walk from the canal path up Warehouse Lane. After 50yds turn right and walk through a mill yard to join Station Road, where you walk left. Turn right between numbers 24 and 26 to take the path that leads between the back gardens of these houses. As you emerge onto Reedymoor Lane you can glimpse Blacko Tower on your right. Bear left until you see an opening on your right called Waller Hill, named after the wallers who built the canal embankment. This took many years, and of a number of shanty towns that grew up, one was here.

Keep left and pass Edwins Villa on your left. Carry straight on along a well-defined path through newish houses on Sycamore Rise. As you pass over Alma Avenue the path descends to the side of Foulridge Lower Reservoir, known by the romantic name of Lake Burwain. It was constructed in 1793 as a feeder for the canal. Turn right along another good path that skirts the edge of the lake. Look right to see, in the adjoining pasture, a red brick chimney, a ventilation shaft for the tunnel. During its construction rubble was removed through such shafts and navvies climbed down them to work.

As you walk behind the Lake Burwain Sailing Club Headquarters the path drops away through the car park and joins a minor road. Turn left out of the car park and almost immediately turn right onto a very narrow tarmacked road that leads directly to Holly Bush Farm. Climb steadily uphill, the reinforced track heavily shaded by tall holly trees that thrive in clean air.

At the farm three footpaths meet. Look for a stone drinking trough on your right. Just beyond, turn right and then immediately left, to pass through a hand gate to a narrow shadowed path through more holly. Climb a stile into a pasture and walk ahead with even more holly to the left and pasture to the right. At the end of the hedge continue to a stile at the end of another hedge coming in on your right. Stride on, with a wall to your left, and continue to pass through a gate to the right of the outbuildings of Whitemoor Riding Centre. Walk by the stables, turn left and pass through a gate on your right. Turn right and walk round the end of the outbuildings to join Standing Stone Lane.

Turn left to walk to the bend in the lane and take the narrow road on the right, signposted Gisburn Track, to walk the walled way. Continue past Brown House (1810) and Green Bank Farm. Beyond Peel's House, take the signposted Pendle Way on your right, passing through a kissing gate onto White Moor. Continue, with the wall to your left, over the heather moorland, from where you have the most magnificent views over to the moors of Thornton, Bleara, Roger and Kelbrook. Below to the right lie the Foulridge reservoirs. These, with others, were constructed to feed water into the canal, which at this summit level was always short of water in dry summers.

Beyond the gate, continue along the walled way over the high moorland. Look for a pair of bullfinches in the small larch plantation to the right. Walk on to take a stone stepped stile on the right. It has a Pendle Way signpost. Go on along a track over the moorland to pass through a gate. Grouse call from the rough pasture to the left. Continue on the steadily descending way. Take a waymarked stepped stile to the left of the next gate and walk another walled track. Continue downhill to straddle the stile at Copy Nook Farm. From here, on a good day, you can see Ingleborough, Pen-y-ghent and Whernside.

Walk down the reinforced track to the side of Fanny Grey's public house. Turn right in front of the inn, cross the road (High Lane) and take the signposted stile on your left. Drop down the slope towards Booth House Farm and the boundary wall to take the gate on your left. From the gate, stroll ahead through a pasture full of sheep and lambs to a stile in the right corner. Beyond, bear slightly left before continuing ahead to pass to the left of a house and a terrace of houses named Park Close.

Turn right onto the road to Salterforth and almost immediately take

Canada Geese in V formation

the signposted footpath on the left. Walk through pleasing woodland, which now clothes a disused quarry. Climb the rough stepped way and then the stile out of the trees and walk on. Take an easy-to-miss gap stile on the right, 100yds beyond the start of a wall on your right. Drop downhill, with a wall to your left, and then descend to a gap stile to the left of a tiny stone building. Walk ahead to a stile which gives access to a track to pass a house on your right. Join its access track, which leads to the road. Turn left and cross Salterforth Bridge (151) to the Anchor Inn, seen on walk 15. The inn was there before the canal was cut. Then the door was blocked off by the embankment and now you drink in what were once the bedrooms, the ground floor becoming cellars!

Join the towpath and walk due south, with the placid waterway to your right. Between the two pleasing stone bridges, Hatters (150) and Mill Hill (149), stands County Brook Mill beside the little County Brook, so called because it was once the boundary between Lancashire and Yorkshire. The brook carries water from the White Moor Reservoir to replenish the canal. Here a milepost tells you that you are $44^{1/4}$ miles from Leeds and 83 miles from Liverpool. Pass under Dauber's Bridge (147). Canada geese fly overhead in chevron formation. Continue past a colourful mooring and walk on into Foulridge to rejoin your car.

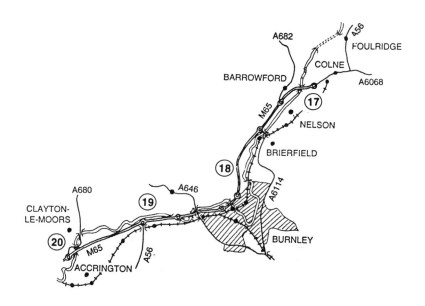

Dipper on rock in icy stream

75

Packhorse Bridge, Higherford

Walk 17: Circular walk from Barrowford

Distance: 10¹/₂ miles
Time: 5 hours
Maps: OS Pathfinder 681 SD 83/93 Burnley
             670 SD 84/94 Barnoldswick and Earby
Terrain: Easy walking all the way.

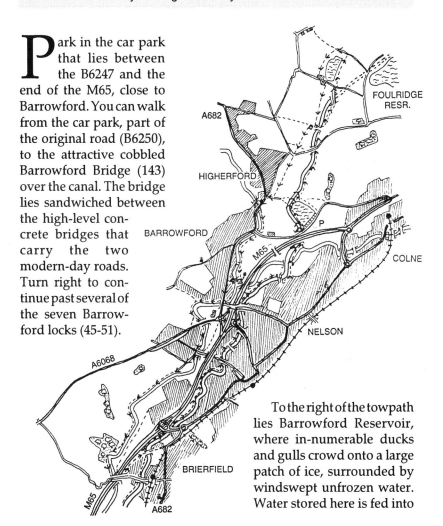

Park in the car park that lies between the B6247 and the end of the M65, close to Barrowford. You can walk from the car park, part of the original road (B6250), to the attractive cobbled Barrowford Bridge (143) over the canal. The bridge lies sandwiched between the high-level concrete bridges that carry the two modern-day roads. Turn right to continue past several of the seven Barrowford locks (45-51).

To the right of the towpath lies Barrowford Reservoir, where in-numerable ducks and gulls crowd onto a large patch of ice, surrounded by windswept unfrozen water. Water stored here is fed into the Lancashire part of the canal.

Walk on to the next lock, the sixth, where there is another parking area and from where there is a good view of Stansfield Tower on Blacko Hill, built in 1890 by Jonathan Stansfield. The final lock is the canal summit at 487$^{1/}$2ft above sea level. By it stands the lock keeper's delightful cottage, beside which several boats are moored. Stroll on to pass under the pleasing Blakey Bridge (144), with pleasant countryside stretching away on either side. To the right flows the narrow Wanless Water. Continue along the lovely tree-lined way beyond Wanless Bridge (145), past a milepost which tells you that you are 81 miles from Liverpool and 46$^{1/}$4 miles from Leeds.

All too soon you come to the south-western end of Foulridge tunnel. There is no continuing towpath and boats were "legged through" until 1880. Today the passage of boats is controlled by traffic lights, and times are displayed on a noticeboard. Cross over the top of the tunnel and then follow a track across a bridge over the Wanless. At the Pendle Way sign turn left to cross the Wanless again and into a hedged lane. Almost immediately take a stone stepped stile on the right. Climb the slope to ascend several steps, to the side of the charming small Slipper Hill Reservoir. Here directors of the canal company had a shooting and fishing lodge.

Walk right (north) beside the tranquil water and at the end of the path pass through a gap stile and walk between cypress and holly to cross another stile. Turn left, pass through the gate and walk up the holly-lined track to Holly Bush Farm. Continue ahead to pass, on your left, a dwelling and its garden. On your right is a holly hedge. Climb the stile and continue along the stiled way above the reservoir, a pale gold in the wintry sun. You reach a waymarked stile in the right corner but do not cross it. Instead walk, right, up the slope to another waymarked stile. Turn left as directed by the waymark to a stile to the right of the corner ahead. (The route is not the same as on the OS map - follow the arrows.)

Continue to a lane ahead. Turn left and drop downhill to take the second footbridge, waymarked, on the right. Continue ahead along the way that keeps to the right of Hawthorn Bank. Stride on to a stile in the left corner. Still the boundary hedges are of holly, which thrives in the pollution-free air. Pass through the gap in the left corner of the field and continue in the same general direction, now with the hedge to your right. Here a charm of goldfinches feeds on a clump of burdock.

Pass through a gated gap stile in the right corner of the pasture and stride ahead to pass through a gate in the left-hand end of the wall. Walk ahead, with the wall to your right, and continue down the track towards Wanless Farm. Just before the gate look for the gap stile on the right - marked footpath but difficult to spot. Follow the waymarks right through gaps and then walk right, up a rocky track to an easy-to-miss waymarked stile, up the bank, now on your left.

Beyond, walk ahead with the wall to your right to a stile in the right corner. Go on to the next stile and then immediately take another on your right. Stride in the same general direction, now with the wall to your left, to walk to the road. Turn left and take a stile on your right to dawdle ahead to a gap stile to the left of a house named Ralph Laithe. From here you can see the frowning face of Pendle Hill.

Pass through the kissing gate in the right corner and walk ahead to an exit from the pasture, left, at the end of the wall into the unmade Grange Avenue. Head on to turn right into Francis Avenue and then left to walk the A682 towards Barrowford. Look for the gap stile at the start of Higherford Bridge, which gives access to the footpath you take to walk beside Pendle Water. First you may wish to walk the elegant packhorse bridge which lies upstream. John Wesley, in the 18th century, preached from here to the folk of Barrowford.

Walk ahead, with the chattering water to your right, to cross the road to visit Pendle heritage centre. It is housed in Park Hill, once the home of the Bannister family whose best known member is Roger, the four-minute miler. Here you can obtain coffee and lunches (closed only on Christmas Day). You can visit an 18th-century walled garden, a cruck barn and a toll house and you may like to browse in the giftshop and the bookshop.

Return to the side of the river and continue along its bank through a park and recreation ground. Once beyond the swings and roundabouts take the bridge over the Pendle and walk ahead along Wilton Street. Cross the busy road and turn left to walk to the bridge over the Pendle - now wider and faster-flowing, having been joined by Colne Water. Do not cross the bridge but turn right to walk Calder Vale, with Nelson College on the other bank of the river. Continue past Calder Vale mill and the one-time Lower Clough mill. Pass through a kissing gate to walk beside the river. Pass through the next kissing gate and under the road bridge, where a dipper sings cheerfully on a rock.

Go ahead with, to your left, first the river and then the pleasant Victoria Park, with its large lake. Continue along Park Avenue, which is at first metalled and then becomes an unmade road. Pass through a stile, beside a gate marked private road (footpath only) into rolling pastures. Across the river lie the busy mills of Nelson. From now on continue on the stiled and gated way beside Pendle Water, following the blue-flagged way.

Where the river makes a wide arc, right, take the grassy track across the arc to walk through beech woodland to join the road. To your left lies a spectacular weir just before the well-proportioned Quaker Bridge. Walk on to cross the bridge and turn right beyond it, to pass under a modern road bridge. (You walk this part of the route in walk 18.) Climb the steps, with the M65 road bridge beyond, and continue right and left to walk through Dawson's Conifers. Bear left between outbuildings to walk a fenced track to a stile into a pasture. Climb the next stile into woodland and ascend through trees to join the canal towpath at Clogger Bridge (138), under which you pass.

Now the towpath takes you on through the mills of Nelson, past steepish streets leading down to the winding waterway. A milepost says that it is 78 miles from Liverpool and $49^{1/4}$ from Leeds. Continue past the old canal company warehouse. Pussy willow, brilliant with silvery buds, edges the way and in the distance lie the surrounding hills.

Then beyond Hodge Bank Bridge (141D) you begin to leave industrialisation behind and on either side are many allotments. Colne Water flows between the cut and the motorway. Pass under the sturdy Swinden Changeline Bridge (142) and then climb up to cross it to join the continuing towpath on the other bank. Follow the splendid curving waterway to cross the three-arched Swinden aqueduct over Colne Water and on to the first of the Barrowford locks. Pass under Barrowford Locks Bridge (142A) to the sturdy Barrowford Road Bridge (143). The car park lies to the right.

The canal at Nelson in the snow

Walk 18: Circular walk from Burnley via Brierfield

Distance:	8 miles
Time:	4 hours
Map:	OS Pathfinder 681 SD 83/93 Burnley
Terrain:	Easy walking all the way.

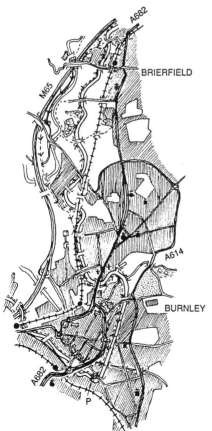

Park in the large car park at Finsley Gate, under the flyover, ¹/₄mile due south of Burnley Town Hall. Walk south up a narrow path through a small lawned area to reach the towpath, where you turn left. Ahead stands the huge banded chimney of a shoe factory, and beyond is an enclosed walkway over the canal.

Next on the towpath is an information board. It tells you about Finsley Gate boatyard which lies on the opposite bank. Boatmen have pulled into the wharves and tied up their barges for overnight maintenance or for more substantial repairs for nearly 200 years. A swing bridge - its keeper's cottage and garden nearby - operated until 1885, when it was replaced by the splendid cast iron Finsley Gate Bridge (130E). The canal company had to win the support of local landowners when planning routes. Significant opposition could hold up a project for years or force an expensive deviation. One common arrangement was for the company to build a swing

Brun Aqueduct, Burnley

82

*Limekilns,
Sainsbury's
car park,
Burnley*

bridge where the canal divided a landowner's property or cut off a part of a town.

Head on along the towpath to pass under bridge 130E and begin the walk along the "straight mile" - actually $^3/_4$ mile. Here the canal is carried on a 60ft embankment high above the town. To the right innumerable streets stretch away in pleasing uniformity. Above the houses tower the lights of the football ground. Beyond lie the snow-dusted slopes of Worsthorne Moor. To the left, steps lead down to Sainsbury's car park. Look for two well-preserved limekilns built into the embankment. Lime was in great demand for mortar for building houses and mills in the rapidly expanding town. Beyond is the green copper dome of the town hall.

Look for the loading crane on the opposite bank, close to picnic tables used by the owners of boats that moor along the embankment. In February the canal can freeze and the powdering of snow upon the ice is scored with skid marks made by flocks of ducks as they land. Webbed footprints criss-cross the ice.

Pass under Godley Bridge (130H) and suddenly, at the end of the long straight stretch, the canal begins to curve and pass between trees. Those on your left skirt the extensive and attractive Thompson Park, given to the city by a mill owner of that name. To the right was a brickworks and Bank Hall Colliery, which was closed in the 1970s. The site has been pleasingly landscaped, the waste from the mine hidden beneath a mantle of grass. Cross the sturdy two-arched aqueduct over the River Brun, from which Burnley's name originates. The railway from the colliery also passed below the bridge.

A milestone tells you that you are 53$^1/_4$ miles from Leeds and 74 miles from Liverpool. Stroll on along the bank, where blue tits call from trees.

Now you pass houses on both sides as you continue below Colne Road Bridge (131) and Old Hall Bridge (131B). Carry on past several mills on the right, one with a pale-coloured stone chimney, and a gasholder on the left. Ahead lies the winding gear of another disused mine and, beyond, the austere face of Pendle Hill, softened with a crown of snow.

At bridge 132A a moorhen starts off across the ice for the security of some willows. Stride the bend, which swings right. More willow and silver birch line the edges of the waterway. Continue along the easy-to-walk towpath past more mills. Then you move out into the gentle countryside, with its small clumps of trees, hedgerows and pastures.

At Hawks House Bridge (136) there is a wooden seat, which in February catches the midday sun. Sit and watch a crowd of mallards standing on ice an inch or two below the surface of the water, the bitter weather seeming to remove all the aggression usually shown by males to each other in close proximity.

Stroll on below the bridge to pass another mill with a canopy for dry-loading boats in days gone by. Pass below Lob Lane Bridge (137) and then the Smith and Nephew factory, which has another canopy and a loading beam. Pass a second gasholder and then woodland on the left. Just before Clogger Bridge (138) leave the towpath, left, and immediately turn left to walk through birch and alder, the latter heavy with catkins.

The path descends right to a stile. Beyond walk through a pasture to the next stile and then stride on along a metalled lane, walking through Dawson's Conifers. At the lane end, bear right and then left to descend steps to the side of fast-flowing Pendle Water. Walk right under the motorway and ahead you can see the double-arched stone bridge over the river. What a lovely corner this must have been before the M65 strode overhead. Cross the stone bridge and look upstream to see a weir over which the beck descends in silvery haste.

Turn left to return under the motorway bridge and walk on beside the hurrying river, where green plover and fieldfare feed in nearby pastures, unconcerned by the traffic on the busy road. Look here for a kingfisher on bare twigs that overhang the Pendle. It moves into the banking, where perhaps it is looking for a suitable hole for its eggs. It flies upstream a short distance and then returns, it too unworried by the noisy traffic.

Beyond the stile, remain on the same side of the river to pass the 18th-century cottage, Pendale (Holme End Farm on the OS map). This area was known as Jack Moore's Monkey. Here Burnley folk would cross the canal and descend the lane to enjoy snacks provided by Jack Moore and view his monkey in its cage. Holidaymakers enjoyed donkey rides and swing boats.

At the track end, turn right and ascend the concrete steps that climb up left to Greenhead Lane, which you cross. Descend the signposted steps on the other side and head across the pasture to the side of the motorway. Walk on in the same general direction. Here a snipe takes off after feeding in the ooze. Look left to see where you walked earlier along the canal.

Climb the stile and go on, ignoring the footpath over the motorway. Look for the next stile in the far left corner and beyond it pass through a gap in the wire fence, now on your right. Follow the hedge on your right and where it ends take another stile. Drop downhill, beside the motorway, to cross yet another stile. Turn left onto a road, and then immediately right to take a footpath, signposted Pendle Water, 250yds ahead. Stride on along a fenced path to a footbridge over the river once again. Beyond, walk the right edge of beech woodland, part of the Woodland Trust, where visitors are welcome to walk.

At the next signpost, turn left and then right. Look for the signposted slope, and then steps, by which you rejoin the towpath. A hundred yards along, leave the towpath, drop down a slope and continue ahead along a narrow path through a large rough area of pasture. This leads you to the side of the railway and the gasholder is prominent on your right. Descend left to pass under the railway to rejoin the towpath by the mill with the pale stone chimney passed earlier.

Walk right, back along the towpath, to Burnley, to rejoin your car.

Mallard on the ice

Manchester Road Wharf, Burnley

Walk 19: Linear walk through Burnley

Distance:	4 miles
Time:	2 hours
Map:	OS Pathfinder 681 SD 83/93 Burnley
Terrain:	Easy walking all the way.

Park in the large car park at Finsley Gate, under the flyover, ¹/₄ mile due south of Burnley Town Hall. Walk south up a narrow path through a small lawned area to reach the towpath, where you turn right. From now on much of the walk takes you through Burnley's 19th-century industrial past. It was once cotton capital of the world, where 100,000 looms wove day and night.

Pass under bridge 130C and walk on beside the wide placid cut. From the towpath you can see the encircling hills, pale green in the early spring sunshine. Look here, along the near edge of the waterway, under a wide concrete flyover, for a narrow cobbled incline sloping into the water, called a "dog wash". Here horses that had fallen could, without injury, regain the towpath.

Next you reach the conservation area known as the Weavers' Triangle, where former spinning mills, weaving sheds and foundries crowd the banks of the waterway. In the foundries steam engines and looms were made. To visit the museum in the old toll house, and the visitors' centre, leave the towpath by Manchester Road Bridge (130B), and walk to the right.

Pass Clocktower Mill, a mule spinning mill begun in 1840. Beyond Sandygate Bridge (130), and on the opposite bank, stands Slater Terrace,

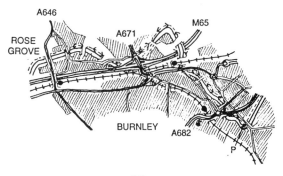

87

in use from 1840. Here workers were housed in two storeys above a warehouse, which stands at water level. Behind, a huge chimney, encircled with red bands, rears upwards. Beyond the terrace lies another mill with a round squat chimney and an ornate square tower, both part of Victoria Mill and Throstle Spinning Mill, begun in 1855. Here blue tits chatter in a solitary pussy willow laden with silvery flowers.

Continue below Mitre Bridge (129B) to walk through a small green "lung", with a grassy area on either side, where willows grow. Beyond the next bridge (129A) an information board explains that the area is part of Lancashire Tree Aid. The planting of the many birches, alders and conifers raised money for a forestry project in Nepal. Climb through the trees to the top of the slope for a grand view of the outskirts of Burnley, with the huge bulk of Pendle Hill leaning benevolently over the sprawling town.

Slater's Terrace, Burnley

Cross a narrow aqueduct over the M65. Close by is Burnley Barracks station. Here three forms of transport come dramatically close. And then you approach the entrance to Gannow Tunnel, 559yds long, where masons' marks

88

adorn the sides of its portal. As there is no towpath the barges would have been "legged through" by the boatmen. The horses were led along Boathorse Lane, and that is the route by which this walk continues.

Leave the towpath and stand above the tunnel (128) to look down on the pleasing winding way of the canal. Cross the road and walk ahead, up the lane, through Whittlefield recreation ground, from where there is a glorious view of Lancashire. At the corner of the Imperial Cinema continue ahead to a busy road. Take the underpass, on your right, to enter a grassed garden with many bushes and a seat. In spite of the traffic all round, this is a good spot for a pause.

To regain the towpath, leave by the Gannow Lane exit and turn left to pass below the motorway. Turn right to the side of the canal where it emerges from the tunnel (still bridge 128). Here the many masons' marks surround the arch. Walk on, with the railway to your left, to pass again under the motorway and its sliproad. Ash and willow flourish on the banks as you pass the Gannow Wharf Inn. Swans swim serenely and mallards indulge in constant squabbling.

As you approach Rose Grove, once a small mill village, now swallowed by Burnley, you can see countryside stretching away to the foot of Pendle Hill. Look for the damaged milepost which tells you that you are 71 miles from Liverpool. Pass below Maden Fold Bridge (127) and beside the Imperial Mill built in 1905 to Dugdale Bridge (126A). Leave the towpath and cross the waterway, passing, on your right, British Waterways' new leisure centre, housed in a restored mill. Continue past Rose Grove library. On your left lies Harling Street with its large blue "P". This is your parking place for the next walk.

To rejoin your car, return along the towpath back through Burnley. Or use Burnley and Pendle transport, bus 50, to return to Finsley Gate (enquiries 01282 425244).

Swans

89

Flagged path, Clayton-le-Moors

Walk 20: Circular walk from Lowerhouse on the outskirts of Burnley

Distance:	11 miles
Time:	5-6 hours
Maps:	OS Pathfinder 680 SD 63/73 Longridge and Great Harwood 681 SD 83/93 Burnley
Terrain:	Easy walking all the way.

P ark in Harling Road (clearly signposted with a blue "P") south of Lowerhouse Bridge (126A). On some maps the latter is named Dugdale Bridge after the Dugdale family who owned local cotton mills, now demolished. Return to the bridge and drop down to the towpath, passing under the bridge. On the opposite bank stands the new Waterways Wharf.

Stride below Liverpool Road Bridge (126) and then on beneath a series of bridges where the canal passes beneath the railway and the motorway. A milestone tells you that your are $57^{1/4}$ miles from Leeds and 70 from Liverpool. Dog's mercury, now in green flower, thrusts upwards through the lifeless wintry vegetation. Then the canal passes back under the motorway once again and continues through pleasing pastures to Knott's Bridge (123). This pleasant stretch of the cut is lined with alders and willows.

Stride on to the white railed overflow and leave the towpath by a footpath that passes through rough pasture and bushes. A factory lies to the right. Ahead lies Padiham and, beyond, the green slopes of Pendle

Clough Bank Bridge

Hill. At a tarmac road, turn left and walk to the crossroads. Continue ahead along a narrow hedged lane towards Castle Clough Farm, where dandelions are in flower. Enjoy this quiet corner while walking past Castle

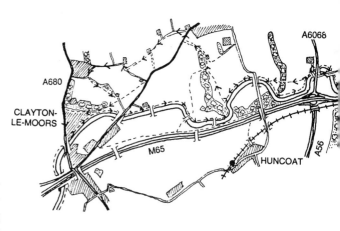

Clough Mill (1846). Ascend the hill, where ewes anxiously watch over their gambolling lambs. Look for the leaves of wild garlic covering the banks.

At the end of the lane, cross the stile to rejoin the towpath and turn right to pass under Higher Shuttleworth Bridge (120). (Because of the new by-pass the OS map route is now out of date.) On the opposite bank stands Shuttleworth House, a gracious white-painted dwelling. Dawdle along the towpath to pass under the by-pass and take the waymarked stile just before the gritstone Shuttleworth Hall Bridge (119). Stride the raised, reinforced track, to a stile and, beyond, to the front of Shuttleworth Hall, which is shaded by tall beech. The hall is a substantial 17th-century house with mullioned windows, painted red.

Return along the track to cross a stile on the right, just before the canal bridge. Walk ahead, bearing slightly to the right, to a metal gate close to the foot of a pylon. Go ahead from the gate (due west) to a footbridge over Shorten Brook. Beyond continue with the fence to the left to a stile on the left, in the corner, which you cross. Carry on with the fence to your right, serenaded as you go by skylarks, to a stile onto the canal embankment. Turn right and follow the cut as it makes a wide curve to the left. From the towpath there is a glorious view ahead of Longridge Fell and beyond. Pass under the attractive Altham Bridge (118), which has an inviting stone seat on its west side. This was a stopping point for the packet boat. Away to the south sprawl green slopes with jagged tops and grassed-over spoil heaps - Great Hameldon (1325ft) and Hameldon Hill (1300ft).

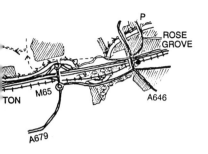

Where the canal swings sharp left, walk ahead into woodland that clothes the sides of Clough Brook. Follow the way as it bears right and keep to the right of several ruined buildings to stroll on an old track, with hawthorns first on the right and then on the left. Go on to a stile beside a gate, with the roof of an industrial unit just visible on the right and woodland to the left. Among the trees are several old fenced mine shafts.

Where the track swings right, take the gate on the left. Walk ahead in the same general direction, through celandines. Keep parallel with the fence on your right, to a sturdy stile to the left of a garage and right of a picturesque cottage named The Old Engine. Here, in this glorious wooded hollow, an engine once pumped water out of the mines in the woodland about Clough Brook. Look over the wall of the lane to see the pretty stream, where you might glimpse a kingfisher.

Follow the lane to its end and cross Burnley Road. Walk right to take a signposted track on the left, just before the cottages at Syke Side. Where the good track swings sharp right, take the stile on the left and walk ahead through a pasture to a stile beside a gate. Away to the right you can see the elegant Whalley viaduct. Pass through the next two stiles and stride on along a delightful hedged grassy way, passing Lower Moor Side. At the end, turn right onto a reinforced cart track and follow it through a small cluster of dwellings as it swings left. Walk on with the high wall of Clayton Hall to the left to take the signposted stile on the right.

Continue in the same general direction with the new houses, a cruck barn and Clayton Hall now to your left. The latter was built in 1772 but became derelict in this century. Today it has been faithfully rebuilt and stands as a fine house in its own parkland. Continue until you reach a row of bungalows, where you turn left before them to walk a sturdy trod of flagstones through woodland. Cross the access track to the hall to continue on the flagged way, with tall trees to the left.

At Butler Cottage turn right and then right again to walk a fenced and walled way to Whalley Road. Turn left to walk into Clayton-le-Moors. Stride the busy road and then drop down left to rejoin the towpath. Leave the bridge (114B) behind you and walk east, soon to leave the houses of the town. Enjoy the glorious distant views as you go. Stride on past Foster's swing bridge (115) and then on to Smith's swing bridge (116). Pass a gaunt derelict house and an ancient ramp, once the wharf and wharf office of the Brick and Lime Company. The attractive Clough Bank Bridge (117) comes next and then you pass the woodland about Clough Brook. Once round the tight left curve you reach the point where you left the canal on the outward part of your walk. From now on follow the towpath back to Lowerhouse Bridge (126A) to rejoin your car, enjoying a wonderful bird's-eye view of where you strolled earlier.

Celandines and dog's mercury

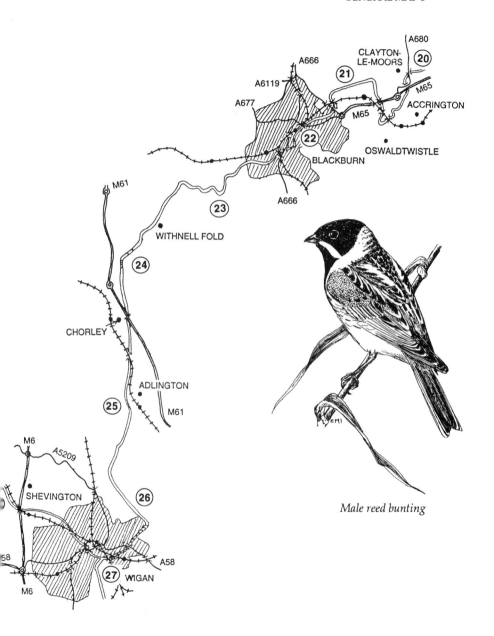

Male reed bunting

Weir on the Hyndburn Brook, below Dunkenhalgh Hall

Walk 21: Circular walk from Clayton-le-Moors

Distance:	12 miles
Time:	5-6 hours
Maps:	OS Pathfinder 680 SD 63/73 Longridge and Great Harwood 689 SD 62/72 Blackburn
Terrain:	Easy walking all the way.

Whalley Road runs through the centre of Clayton-le-Moors. The small car park, well signposted, lies to the west of the main road. After parking, return to the A class road and turn right. One hundred yards on, turn right to join the towpath at Whalley Road Bridge (114B). Walk on (south) along the good towpath to pass a milestone that says that you are 62¹/₄ miles from Leeds. Stride on to pass a new building, which is being constructed on the site of an old cotton mill. In front of it a colourfully painted wall carries the words HALF WAY, indicating you are halfway from Leeds to Liverpool.

At Enfield Changeline Bridge (114A) you cross the canal and continue onwards, now on the opposite bank. The towpath on this stretch of the canal was placed on the eastern bank because the Victorian owner of the

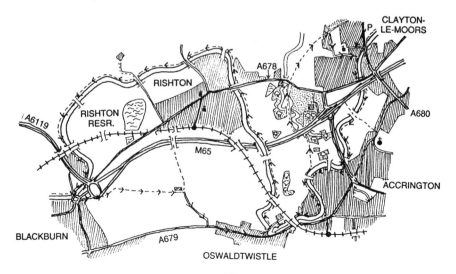

Dunkenhalgh estate, on the western side, feared his deer would be poached by bargees.

Pass under the motorway and continue. Fields stretch away on either bank and there are distant views of the moors. Walk past Riley's swing bridge (114) and then an area of humps and hollows where clay was removed for brick-making. Away on the far side of the canal you can see Dunkenhalgh Hall, now a hotel. A flock of green plovers feed in the nearby pasture, uttering their haunting cries.

Cross a humpbacked bridge over a wharf where barges were tied up to deliver coal. Here an angler delights in having landed a pike - one fewer to prey on the trout and perch.

Pass Church swing bridge (113) and continue into the village of Church, once famous for its printing of calico and its turkey red dye. The industry was developed by the Peel family, who strove hard for the canal to be routed so that it could supply the water needed for their works. Then you come to the parish church of St James, known as Church Kirk, which has many ornate gravestones in the churchyard. It has a 15th-century tower and font but the remainder was built in the 19th century. If the church is open, go inside and enjoy the lovely stained glass, the unusual ceiling and the balcony supported by thin but sturdy pillars.

Return to the towpath and walk on to cross the Church Kirk Changeline Bridge (112). Continue past several mills crowding both sides of the cut.

At the sharp right turn, look for the derelict but still fine wharf, with a central arch, on the opposite bank. Continue under several more bridges until you come to what are known locally as the "fairy caves". This is a series of coke ovens, still in a relatively good state of preservation.

As so often when you walk the Leeds and Liverpool canal, the housing and industrialisation ends abruptly and ahead lie green fields seemingly stretching away to the distant hills.

Here the canal makes a huge loop. Its builders wanted to avoid hilly ground and to meet the wishes of mill owners and of landowners through whose land it passed. Thus, a mile further along the towpath you can look right to see first the coke ovens, then Church Kirk again. Then just before New Barn Bridge (109) look right to see Clayton-le-Moors, which you left an hour or more before. Stride the narrow aqueduct over the motorway with another good view of Dunkenhalgh Hall.

Then the canal makes another great curve, this time around Rishton.

Coke ovens, near Church

Follow the curve north-west and then continue towards Blackburn. This part of the towpath can be muddy after rain. Here a pair of swans comes close to the bank and you are "encouraged on your way" by the aggressive male. Further on a male reed bunting, resplendent in nuptial plumage, flies ahead, settling on the low-growing vegetation at the water's edge.

After passing through more countryside you reach the retail park at Whitebirk, built on the site of Blackburn's coal-fired power station. On the opposite bank sheep graze in a pasture and further on trees line the water. Through them flit a pair of bullfinches. Pass below a huge concrete flyover and continue to Whitebirk Bridge (104B) just beyond a pet-meat store. Climb up the cobbled side of the bridge, cross over the canal and continue to the roundabout. Cross with care and walk the footpath along the side of the slip road, facing traffic coming from the motorway. Continue round the huge roundabout to climb a stile into pastures on your right.

Walk ahead to cross a small stream by a tractor bridge and head to the stile in the right corner, to the left of a little stream. Continue up the slope to the right of Cowhill Fold. Continue on the stiled way in front of the farm, and buildings beyond, to climb the stile at the end of a short track. Drop downhill beside the fence on your right to climb a stile over another fence. Strike diagonally left to climb a stile over the next boundary fence. Turn left and, beyond the next stile, turn right to walk to the road.

Walk left along the main street through West End, Oswaldtwistle. Turn left beyond the Hare and Hounds public house to cross Aspen Bridge (110) to rejoin the towpath. Pass under the bridge. Walk past the coke ovens and stroll on to the Church Kirk Changeline Bridge (112). Do not cross but take the track, fenced with railings, which continues parallel with the waterway. Follow the track as it swings left and then along the track to pass under the motorway.

Enjoy the pleasing way below the stately Dunkenhalgh Hall and beside the gently flowing Hyndburn Brook. At the track end, cross the busy road with care and continue on along the signposted footpath. Follow the track, diverting left and then right to cross the gill where the footbridge has collapsed. Stride on across the stiled pastures to the road. Turn right to walk Charles Street to pass Hyndburn museum and park. Take the continuing footpath and then turn left to walk behind a row of cottages. Head on uphill to join the towpath. Turn left and leave the cut just before Whalley Road Bridge (114B). Turn left onto Whalley Road and turn left again at the car park sign to rejoin your car.

Feral pigeon on a girder

Walk 22: Linear walk through Blackburn

Distance:	8 miles
Time:	4 hours
Map:	OS Pathfinder 689 SD 62/72 Blackburn
Terrain:	Easy walking all the way.

Leave your car in the parking area of Pleasington playing fields in Witton Country Park. The entrance lies off a narrow road on the right (if travelling west), off the A674 at Feniscliffe. Walk back towards the gate to the park and take a footpath on the right. Follow it as it leads diagonally to a narrow road. Walk ahead to the A674, where you turn right to cross the road by the traffic-light controlled crossing. Continue right and almost immediately turn left into the narrow, pathless busy road just before Cherry Tree Station. Walk ahead to drop down left to join the towpath at Cherry Tree Bridge (95) to begin a pleasing linear walk through Blackburn. Continue with the cut to your right.

In 1800 Blackburn was changing from a big village to a small industrial town. The force behind the change was the cotton industry. But at first industry could develop only as fast as packhorses could carry the goods. With the coming of the canal change came

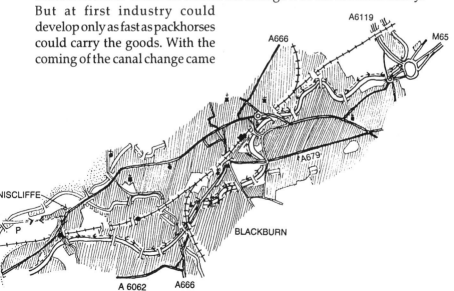

101

Eanan Wharf, Blackburn

faster than anyone could believe. The canal was the motorway of the early 19th century.

Willows and birch, from which great and blue tits call, intermittently line the towpath. This has been pleasingly reinforced and is a joy to walk. Pass, on your right, an old cotton mill with a tall chimney. The mill is now a superstore. Continue under Bower House Fold Bridge (96) and on to Kings Bridge (96A) to walk past The Navigation public house. Pigeons nest in the iron girders of Kings Bridge.

By Moorgate Fold Bridge (96B) coltsfoot brightens the way with yellow flowers; not that the way is dark, because so many of the Victorian mills that cast their deep shadows on the water have been demolished, allowing light to flood into the canal corridor. After passing below the next attractive bridge continue by the Water's Edge public house.

Carry on past a small park and then along a raised embankment from where you have a good view of the pleasant town. Below lies the centre of Blackburn. Rows and rows of houses stretch up the hillside. Beyond lies the open countryside, rolling moors and woods, cradling the town. These hills created the damp atmosphere essential for the production of cotton.

Away to the right of the cut is Blackburn Rovers football ground and, beyond, up on the moors, stands Darwen Tower. Cross the Ewood Aqueduct. It once spanned the River Darwen, which is now culverted below a road. Stroll on past the Canal View public house. Pass under another metal bridge, where more pigeons have taken up residence, to reach the first of Blackburn's six gritstone locks. The locks (52-57) raise the canal to a height of more than 400ft above sea level. To the right stands the Royal Infirmary.

Then the cut makes a large curve to the right in front of The Moorings public house. In front of the pub is a large winding hole, where boats could turn using the power of the wind. Here you leave the towpath by a cobbled slope to cross Bolton Road by bridge 99. Pass through a white-painted metal gate to rejoin the way in front of the lock keeper's cottage, where there is another lock. Before the next lock, reached by a cobbled way, is another large winding hole.

Continue under Hall Street Bridge (99A) and Highfield Road Bridge (100) to cross a narrow road to rejoin the towpath. Pass Nova Scotia Mill and walk under Grimshaw Park Bridge (101). Notice the attractive signposts and lampposts along the way. Enjoy more good views of the town. Look on the stone of Brewery Bridge (102) for the deep indentations

Daisyfield Mill, Blackburn

caused by the ropes attached to the horses pulling the boats. A pleasing sitting area might encourage you to watch the world go by for a short time. And then pass under Audley Bridge (102A) and past the Barge Inn on the opposite bank. Willows and birch grow here. Continue past a "dog wash" and then Blackburn Station and ahead lies the new town hall, a tall glass and concrete building contrasting with Blackburn's gracious cathedral, beside it.

Continue along the high-level way with a grandstand view of Blackburn's many church towers and chimneys. After Cicely Bridge (103) you pass Tommy Ball's shoe emporium. And then a red and black iron bridge spans the cut. Beyond lie the elegant canopied Eanam Wharf, once a canal depot and now a conference centre, and the Wharf public house. Go inside and enjoy the well-arranged display boards telling of the development of the waterway. You are now 57 miles from Liverpool.

Just before Paradise Bridge (103B) is a disused Georgian flour mill that still has inlets for water to be used in the processes. Pass another "dog wash". Along this part of the canal several grain mills were devoted to producing flour to feed the ever-increasing population of the cotton town.

Then you come to Daisyfield Mill, another old grain mill, now magnificently refurbished, part of it housing Granada TV. Near Sour Milk Hall Bridge (104) is a large bowling alley in front of which are planted many horse-chestnut trees. Beyond lies a cotton spinning mill. Continue under Greenbank Bridge (104A) and Whitebirk Bridge (104B). (This is where you end the canal part of walk 21.)

As this is a linear walk, return along the towpath to rejoin your car. Or you may wish to use the 73 bus into the centre of Blackburn and then the 123 to Feniscliffe using Ribble buses (enquiries 01254 51236).

Walk 23: Circular walk from Feniscliffe via Withnell Fold

Distance:	9¹/₂ miles
Time:	4-5 hours
Map:	OS Pathfinder 689 SD 62/72 Blackburn
Terrain:	Easy walking all the way.

Park in the well-signposted Pleasington playing fields (see walk 22), which lie west of the A674 on the western edge of Blackburn. Walk back towards the entrance and leave the road by a narrow path to the right that leads across rough ground, through broom, birch and heather towards houses at Feniscliffe. Climb the steps out of the playing fields into Geddes Street and walk ahead to the A674, which you cross by the pedestrian crossing. Turn right and then left into Green Lane, following the direction for Cherry Tree Station. Cross the railway bridge and then drop down right to the towpath at Cherry Tree Bridge (95).

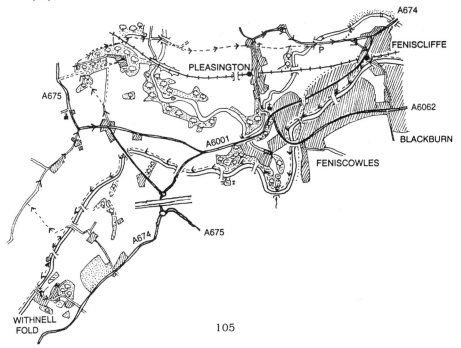

Pleasington Priory

Walk west, away from Blackburn, to pass Cherry Tree machine mill. Stride on. Enjoy the gardens of the houses on the far bank. These slope down to the cut, and are full of spring flowers. Beyond Livesey Hall Bridge (94) is an old mill that used to make bits and pieces for the textile industry and close by are gritstone abutments, remnants of an iron bridge that carried a now-dismantled railway.

Pass under Feniscowles Bridge (93B), where newly built houses are gradually encroaching on the pastures beside the waterway. Further on look for a narrow stone ledge, all that remains of a swing bridge that once carried a 19th-century road. Now the towpath leads you through delightful woodland on both sides of the cut, where a spotted woodpecker chippers. Look here for a kingfisher that rears its brood a foot above the water on the opposite bank. Dawdle on past a paper mill, which is almost hidden from view by trees and a fence. Look for the many iron rings on the towpath where barges would have tied up when delivering to the mill.

Continue beneath Stanworth Bridge (93), a metal bridge painted black and white, supported on stone abutments. Enjoy this lovely tranquil way, which at the time of writing has not been polluted by the noise of the approaching M56. Look back for a pleasing view of the bridge and two mill chimneys rearing above the trees. On the far bank is a small grassy banked reservoir which once supplied Feniscowles with all its water.

Pass below Millfield Bridge (92) and look for swallows and grey wagtails, pairs of both birds swooping over the still water. Then continue beneath Finnington Bridge (91B). Stroll on through the rolling

Swallows

pastures. Here on the far bank the waterway has been reinforced with stone and in these a pair of sandpipers rears its brood. Soon the towpath is lined with brightly coloured boats as you approach Riley Green Bridge (91A), where you will find North West Narrow Boatyard.

Stroll on past anglers who fish for bream, carp, tench and perch. Here the new motorway will stride the canal. Walk on through this glorious part of Lancashire to pass under the three stone Ollerton Bridges, numbers 3, 2 and 1 (91, 90 and 89). This part of the canal leads into the village of Withnell Fold. Cross the bridge (88) and walk the cobbled way into the small village, which was built to house workers at the paper mills beside the canal, where banknote paper was made. Look for the terraced cottages grouped on three sides of a square, with a set of stocks on the fourth. Sit in the memorial gardens, pleasingly landscaped in what was once the lodge (a reservoir of water) for the mill.

Return over the bridge and walk back along the towpath to a stile on the left, just before Ollerton Bridge, number 2. Beyond, strike diagonally left, keeping to the right of a small flooded area, the haunt of oystercatchers, redshanks, green plover and dozens of swallows flying low over the water. Cross the footbridge over Whaves's Brook and continue uphill, keeping close to the hedge on your left. Climb the signposted stile. Walk right along Marsh Lane to pass Leigh Farm and on to where the motorway will cut through the lovely countryside.

At the T-junction, continue ahead to pass Head-o'-the-Marsh Farm and then Moss Farm. At the next T-junction, cross the road, turn right and walk into Riley Green. Just before the Royal Oak Hotel, turn left to take the signposted footpath. Cross two ladder stiles, and then continue uphill to climb two more ladder stiles to a track. To the right stands the dramatic castellated Hoghton Tower, built by Thomas Hoghton in 1565. It is set on a hill - the south-westerly tip of the Pendle range. The house is a delight and well worth a visit.

At the track, walk ahead and then drop down the slope to cross the main access track to the tower. Continue along a lane to pass several estate houses. Go on the delightful stiled way, with the wall of the tower to your right. Climb the stile ahead, where two walls meet, into glorious woodland. At the signpost, drop down the slope to cross, with care, the railway line. Bear slightly right to a stile and, beyond, descend the continuing grassy slope to climb two stiles to a narrow lane.

Stride ahead down a track to the right of a farm to cross the River Darwen. Look right to see an elegant viaduct rising above the tops of the trees that clothe the slopes on which Hoghton Tower stands. Walk ahead from the bridge and, where the track comes beside a wall, cross the stile on your right. Dawdle along the lovely path, which for a short distance edges the golf course, passing through birch, heather and oak. Many spring migrants call from the bushes and from the pastures come the bubbling calls of curlews. Stroll on along the stiled way, with no directions required, until you reach Pleasington and its magnificent Priory church.

Turn left along Sandy Lane and take the signposted Old Hall Lane on the right. Continue ahead to pass, on your left, the charming Old Hall Farm. Turn right at the cemetery road and follow the track to rejoin your car.

Viaduct over the River Darwen, below Hoghton Tower

Withnell Fold

Walk 24: Circular walk from Chorley

Distance:	10½ miles
Time:	5-6 hours
Maps:	OS Pathfinder 699 SD 41/51 Chorley
	689 SD 62/72 Blackburn
	688 SD 42/52 Preston (South) & Leyland
Terrain:	Easy walking all the way.

P ark in the large car park of the Hop Pocket public house, Chorley
Moor, where the landlord, Ian Mckechnie, welcomes walkers -
asking them just to mention that they are there. Walk left out of
the car park, cross the busy road and continue ahead along Carr Lane,
which is a no-through road. Cross, with care, the A6 and stride on along
Hoggs Lane, a hedged track, where every hawthorn bush seems to have
its own resident spring migrant. Pass under the lofty viaduct and stroll
to the towpath. Turn left and walk the pleasing way as the houses of
Chorley come into view.

Pass a one-time cotton mill that has a copper dome with the date 1906
below it. Pass under Cowling Bridge (75A) from where a sandpiper flies
ahead along the waterway. Carry on past Matthew Brown's brewery to
walk the newly restored towpath. The bed of the canal has had some
restoration work done too. A synthetic lining has been put in place.

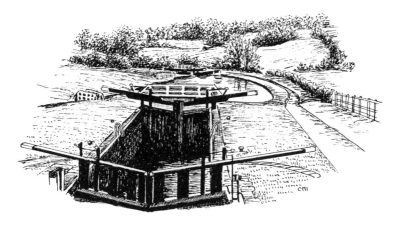

Johnson's Hillock Locks

Cross a sturdy aqueduct over a fast-flowing stream and continue to Cross Hall Bridge (76). Leave the towpath here and cross over the canal. As you walk on, look right for a good view of the aqueduct recently crossed. Turn left just before the bridge over the M61 and stride the track to pass the remnants of an old mill. Continue to a road and here turn right to cross the motorway. Beyond, continue past a centre for making carpets and

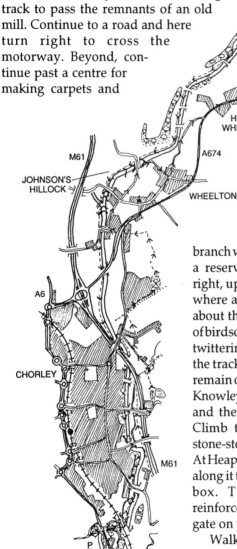

go ahead along a stiled track, with the factory to your left.

Follow the track and take the left branch where it divides. Walk beside a reservoir on your left. To your right, up a grassy bank, lies another where anglers fish. The hedgerows about the stretches of water are full of birdsong and linnets fly overhead, twittering as they go. Head on along the track beside a pretty stream and remain on it as it swings left towards Knowley. Pass Bagganley Lane Farm and then take a stile on the right. Climb the slope to a signposted stone-stepped stile. Beyond, turn left. At Heapey Road cross and walk right along it to just beyond the telephone box. Turn left and walk the reinforced track to a stile beside a gate on your left.

Walk ahead, with a grand bird's-eye view over Chorley. Stride on, leaving the track just before a gate and walk towards a stile, with the hedge and fence to your right. Follow the path as it swings left, downhill, and climbs a signposted stile. Turn right to cross a bridge over a disused railway track. Turn right into Merton Grove and climb the grassy slope on your right just before the first house. Stride the footpath that runs behind the houses. A glorious wooded bank drops steeply down to the bed of the old railway. Comfrey and forget-me-nots flower along the way.

Dawdle along the lovely path, with dramatic views over right to misty hills. Carry on, with a derelict wall to your left, and then drop down a slope to straddle a stile on your left. (Do not descend to the bed of the railway track.) Walk ahead to cross the next stile and, beyond, join a track and follow it as it winds round left beside a pool. The pool is rapidly being colonised by willow, a sanctuary for chiffchaffs, marsh tits and willow warblers.

Stride through the delectable woodland, ignoring a track and path which both lead off left. At the end of the woodland, where the track swings left up the slope to a sand and gravel pit, take a stile on your right and walk over a pasture to cross the next stile. The grassy way soon becomes a clear path and gently climbs to a gap in a hedgerow. Head on over more pasture to pass through a gap in a holly hedge. Beyond, walk left to climb a stile into a small wood, where you turn right at the top of the slope. Follow the track to a division of ways and take the narrower path beside the fence on your right, dropping downhill through the trees. Walk to the left of a wooden shed and then ahead to continue along a narrow path between cypresses that lies to the right of a bungalow and leads to the B6228.

Cross the road, turn right and continue to cross the A674. Walk slightly left to take the old road that cuts off the corner of the road to Whittle-le-Woods. Just before a bridge, turn right to walk Dark Lane. Continue past the stone-mullioned Howard Arms Hotel, built to serve Victorians who wished to make use of the Whittle springs. Beyond, climb the hill and at the T-junction turn right. Almost immediately turn left to walk the pleasant Copthurst Lane to arrive at the Top Lock Bridge (82). Do not cross but turn right to walk beside the Top Lock public house. Stroll on past Wheelton boatyard and then on again to pass the clocktower memorial in the typical Lancashire village of Wheelton.

After exploring the quiet village, turn left to walk up the old Blackburn Road. Stride the continuing track and then the road beyond. You are now high above the canal. Join the Chorley Road and walk on through Higher Wheelton for $^1/_2$ mile - there is a pavement, but walk with care. As you approach the Blackburn Road pumping station, take the acute left turn to walk a reinforced track. Stride the pleasing gated way into the charming village of Withnell Fold (seen on walk 23).

Turn left to walk the cobbled way, passing the stocks on the right, above the memorial gardens, which are laid out in what was once the mill lodge or water store. Follow the road right to pass the mill, with its tall chimney. Cross Withnell Fold Bridge (88) and pass below it to walk the towpath, which is delightfully wooded on both sides. Pass below Jackson's Bridge (87) and Brown House Bridge (86). Their parapets slope steeply from left to right to accommodate the hilly land on the far bank.

Go on through the rolling countryside to pass under Simpson's Fold Bridge (85) and then under the attractive Engine Bridge (84) and Whins Bridge (83). Continue to the top lock (58) of the Johnson's Hillock flight of seven, at which point the canal has been raised 65ft 6in. Stride on along the pleasant, gently descending towpath to cross a metal bridge. Below is a junction of waters where the Leeds and Liverpool Canal connects with the Walton Summit Branch of the Lancaster Canal. The branch line, now blocked off by the M61, connected with the Lancaster Canal via a horse tramway.

Carry on to pass under Moss Lane Bridge (80) and under Knowley Bridge (79). Beyond Botany Bay Bridge (78A) there is a long-term mooring. Legend has it that the area was called Botany Bay because the living conditions were considered as bad as those of the renowned Botany Bay in Australia.

From now on the path is well reinforced and lined with blackthorn in white blossom. Very soon you reach the part of the towpath you walked at the start. Pass under Cowling Bridge (75A) and just before the attractive Barracks Bridge (75) turn right off the towpath. Walk along the path and continue along Hoggs Lane. Pass under the viaduct and stroll on to cross the A6. Continue along Carr Lane and cross the road to rejoin your car at the Hop Pocket.

Common sandpiper

Walk 25: Circular walk from Heath Charnock, south of Chorley

Distance:	10¹/₂ miles
Time:	5-6 hours
Map:	OS Pathfinder 699 SD 41/51 Chorley & Burscough Bridge
	OS 711 SD 40/50 Wigan & Ormskirk
Terrain:	Easy walking all the way.

L and L Cruisers, a boatyard, is found in Burnsall Avenue, Heath Charnock, to the south of Rawlinson Bridge (71), south of Chorley. Park in one of the several laybys on either side of the A6, just north of the boatyard and the bridge. Or, after asking permission in the boatyard shop, use its parking area. Join the towpath and walk south, passing under bridge 71 and Allinson Hall Bridge (70). Here, in spring, the way is lined with hawthorn, bursting into green foliage, and the bushes are full of birdsong. Bluebells and wood sorrel edge the path and blackthorn bushes are in blossom.

Continue past Whitebear Marina. Here, close to Whitebear Bridge (69), a mallard duck anxiously marshals eight ducklings. Stroll on past the Bridge public house and below Red House Bridge (68). Dawdle across an aqueduct over the River Douglas, which flows fast through

Rawlinson Bridge

115

Arley Bridge

glorious woodland far below. From here you can hear the courting calls of curlews in the pastures on either side and the raucous calls of jays from the trees.

Stroll on under Waterhouse Bridge (67) and continue along the towpath through delightful rolling countryside, from where comes the constant serenade of skylarks. Pass under Aberdeen Bridge (66), admiring the pleasing reflection of daffodils in the water, and on to Weavers Bridge (65). Continue past Arley wood, where a mass of wild flowers thrives beneath the birch trees. Walk on beside the golf course to pass the moated Arley Hall, now used as a clubhouse. From the nearby bushes come the calls of the blackcaps.

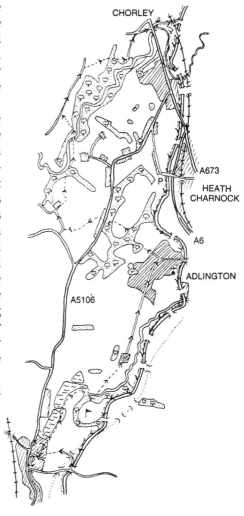

Go on under the attractive Arley Bridge (64) and dawdle along the towpath through more grand deciduous woodland. A milestone tells you that you are 87$^{1}/_{4}$ miles from Leeds and 40 from Liverpool. Cross a high-level iron bridge over a dismantled railway and continue to just before Red Rock Bridge (63). Leave the towpath and walk the unmade road that bears right, going back beside the waterway for a short distance. Then follow it as it swings away from the canal.

Cross the dismantled railway again and continue past an attractive pond with geese and coots. Walk on to a stile to the left of a barn. Beyond, walk ahead, with a fence to the left, and then pass through a gate on your left. Continue downhill to a stile, and then steps, to a road. Turn left to walk beside Coates Vyella dyeworks lodge (store of water). Turn right almost immediately to walk through the buildings of the mill. Turn right and walk, with much care, for 200yds along the Chorley Road to the Visitor Centre at Worthington Lakes. The centre lies off the road in the middle of the car park. The lakes are reservoirs managed by North West Water.

Stride to the right of the centre and bear right to cross the large dam to gain access to the far bank of Worthington Reservoir. Here cowslips flourish. Look for several pairs of great crested grebes which, though already paired, continue their fascinating courtship ritual.

Remain on the same bank and continue on this idyllic walk beside Arley Reservoir. Climb the stile on the right and, ignoring the footbridge on the right, walk on through the trees. Climb the stepped slope into pasture and stroll ahead to Crawshaw Hall. Go on along the access track, then the continuing narrow road (Common End). Then walk along the left pavement of a wider road (The Common) into the village of Adlington. Where the main road bears right, turn left into Sandy Lane. Walk to the two-armed signpost and carry on along a hedged and fenced path, all the way to the Wigan Road, which you cross with care.

Take the gated track opposite and stroll the pleasing way through woodland and pasture to the signposted end. Turn right to walk the lane. At Coppull Hall, turn right into a signposted track. Carry on beside a hedge on your left and then walk across a pasture to the edge of Coppull Hall Wood. Drop down through the trees (the path is indistinct and not signposted) to the path beside the River Yarrow. Turn right and follow the lovely river, upstream, through magnificent woodland. Continue along the stiled way to cross a pasture high above the river to a stile into woodland again. Descend to cross a green metal bridge. Walk ahead to where, almost immediately, you are confronted by two paths; take the left branch. Climb steps out of the trees and, beyond the stile at the top, follow the clear waymarked path to Burgh Lane South, where you turn right.

At the next crossroad, take a gate on the right to walk a reinforced track which keeps to the right of an estate (not on the OS map). At the gated end walk ahead through the houses to continue on an unmade lane to the left of a white cottage. Take the signposted path on the right. Strike across the pasture to a stile to playing fields. Beyond, walk ahead through the fields, with the school to your left and fenced woodland to your right. Where the fence ends, turn right and pass through a gap in the trees to a gated path that runs beside the extensive woodland. At the end of the path, turn left onto a track.

Walk the reinforced way in front of an industrial unit and the NORWEB training centre. Continue along the road and then turn right onto a busy road to pass the Hop Pocket public house (parking place for walk 24). Walk straight on along Carr Lane, cross the A6 and carry on along Hoggs Lane. Pass under the viaduct and dawdle on to the towpath. Turn right and pass under Barracks Bridge (75), where the stonework has many grooves made by the ropes of the horses towing barges. Continue beneath a skew bridge, 74A, which carries the railway, and go on past magnificent bluebell woodland. Pass beneath Ridding Bridge (74) and on to cross the River Yarrow by an aqueduct.

Next you pass under Giles Bridge (73) and then Chorley Road Bridge (72A) followed by Idle Bridge (72). On the struts of the latter a kestrel has built its nest. The next bridge is Rawlinson Bridge (71), where you leave the canal to rejoin your car.

Pair of great crested grebes courting

Worthington Lakes

Walk 26: Circular walk from Worthington Lakes

Distance:	8 miles	
Time:	5 hours	
Maps:	OS Pathfinder	699 SD 41/51 Chorley & Burscough Bridge
		711 SD 40/50 Wigan & Ormskirk
Terrain:	Easy walking all the way.	

P ark in the car park at Worthington Lakes (passed through on walk 25). The lakes are three reservoirs, Worthington, Arley and Adlington, and have supplied drinking water for more than 100 years. There is a visitor centre and toilet facilities. Footpaths lead around the three reservoirs and there are picnic areas and benches.

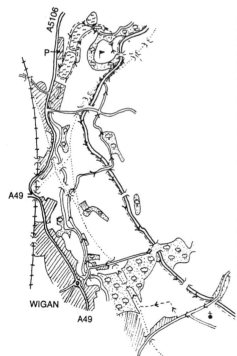

Walk past the chalet classroom and turn right where, in autumn, long trails of wild bryony carry large clusters of red glass-like berries as they clamber over hawthorn and blackberry equally laden with fruit. Cross the dam, colourful with ragwort and knapweed, and enjoy the superb view across the tree-girt tranquil water.

Turn left to walk the good path that runs along the far bank, passing under oaks. Look for a handsome cormorant sitting quite still as it patiently waits for prey, its yellow beak and white cheeks catching the sun. Close by, several pairs of great crested grebe preen and utter their strange banjo-like call. Continue under sycamore and horse-chestnut trees now tinged with browns and golds.

At the far corner of Arley Reservoir, take the stile on the right and continue into glorious woodland. Where the path divides, keep to the upper one to pass through Indian balsam covered with large elegant pink flowers. Here the River Douglas, which rises on Winter Hill and was crossed by an aqueduct south of Adlington, passes under Worthington Lakes by tunnel to emerge beyond.

Follow the path down steps on the right and cross a metal bridge over the river. Stride ahead uphill through the lovely deciduous woodland to Arley golf course. Walk ahead until you reach the wall about the stately clubhouse. Stroll right, keeping the wall to your left until you reach a stile on the right, which gives access to the towpath. Turn right and walk beside the canal, where a milestone states that it is 87 miles to Leeds and 40 to Liverpool. Cross Red Rock aqueduct over the disused Whelly Loop line. Enjoy this reed-fringed stretch of the waterway, where sheep graze on both banks.

Pass under Red Rock Bridge (63) and continue past the Crawford Arms, named after the Crawford family, who lived at nearby Haigh Hall. Continue past moorings and look across right to fields bounded by wooden fences. Beyond you can see rows of Lombardy poplar and on a warm autumn day you feel as if you are in France - where is this elusive place called Wigan?

After Sennicar Bridge (61) great lily pads float along the far side of the canal. And then on the far bank you can see another golf course, this time at Haigh Hall. The Crawfords became very wealthy from the coal found under their land. It was called Cannel, a particularly fine coal, with double the value of ordinary coal. It was used in the production of oil and gas and was so hard that it could be carved. Haigh Hall had a summer house built of it. Saunter on past high stands of bulrushes and then look left on higher ground for a fine view of the hall. On your right is a small pond where the hall's rowing boats were moored. Today it is enjoyed by perch and surrounded by rhododendrons.

Cross a narrow stone bridge over the inflow from the canal to the pond and pass under the fine iron-latticed Haigh Hall Bridge (60). Sheffield Bridge (59B) has timber struts along its side to protect the boats and all about is riotously coloured vegetation. Walk on to pass on the far bank the Bellhouse. In this lived the owner of a large sawmill, now gone, where the canal boats were repaired. Beyond, facing onto Wigan Road, is a private house named the Packet House. Here boats tied up overnight before tackling the long flight of locks down to Wigan.

Bridge, Haigh Hall

There was also a mortuary where people who died in the canal were laid out.

Leave the towpath just before Springs Bridge (59A) and walk right along the Wigan Road. Pass the Crown Hotel and the school. Turn right into an unsignposted wide grassy area between two rows of terraced houses. Pass allotments on the right and through a gap to the right of a large wooden gate. Walk ahead along a fenced way, planted with young trees on either side. This was once the site of a deep coal mine, followed by open cast mining. Now it has been pleasingly landscaped with walkways constructed by the Coal Board.

Where the fenced way divides, bear left and continue to the edge of Bottling Wood. Drop down the slope, close to the continuing fence on the left, and then walk right along part of the disused coal-carrying railway crossed earlier. Continue on the track where it has been cut through rock. Vegetation comes close to the narrow path. Pass under another elegant bridge, part of the Haigh Hall estate, and climb up the slope on your left to join the long-distance footpath, The Douglas Way. Before you continue, step back a very short distance to see the grand bridge that carries a narrow road to the hall. All around are magnificent beech trees with leaves a glowing bronze.

Continue on in the same direction above the disused railway, now very muddy and overgrown. The path continues beyond the woodland beside a hedge on the right where large numbers of fly agaric flourish among the roots of young oak and birch. The path passes through more trees and comes to a stile to the left of a railway bridge. Turn left and walk along the quiet Hall Lane. Take the cobbled short cut down the slope on the left and cross Hall Lane with care.

Turn right into Windgates Road, another quiet lane, to pass the intrusive Douglas Valley Business Park. Continue along the tree-lined unmade Pendlebury Lane. Pass under a railway bridge and look left to see a fine viaduct. Then stroll on along the track to cross the canal by Pendlebury's Bridge (62). Turn left beyond the first house and walk a track past Winstanleys and Bawk House to the road (B5239). Cross with care and take the signposted footpath opposite. Walk to the end of 12 terraced cottages. Once there were three rows, in which miners lived. Turn left and follow the narrow path to the side of the canal. Walk with care along the narrow path and then into woodland close beside the waterway.

Continue to Arley Bridge (64), which you cross. Turn left and almost immediately turn right to follow the wall of Arley Hall once again. At the car park keep straight ahead through an avenue of lime trees. Once inside the woodland, turn right and drop down to cross the bridge. Climb the steps, turn left and walk to the stile. Beyond, walk ahead and return to the car park by walking on the opposite banks of the reservoirs to those taken at the start of the walk.

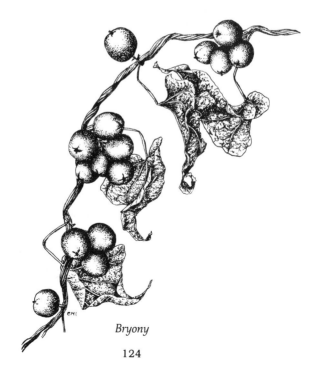

Bryony

124

Walk 27: Linear walk through Wigan

Distance:	5¹/₂ miles
Time:	At least 5 hours if you visit Wigan Pier
Map:	OS Pathfinder 711 SD 40/50 Wigan & Ormskirk
	712 SD 60/70 Bolton (South)
Terrain:	Good walking all the way.

P ark close to the Crown Hotel, just west of Springs Bridge (59A) on the Wigan Road (B5238), the public house passed after leaving the towpath on walk 26. Join the towpath to begin your walk towards Wigan with the canal on your left. Look for the red brick structure on the far bank, a preserved building and all that remains of the great Wigan Coal and Iron Company's works that stretched from the top lock to lock 9. Legend says that at night when all the 10 blast furnaces and nearly 700 coke ovens were working, you could see to read a newspaper in the town.

Ahead is Monk Hall Bridge (59), but before this the canal turns sharp right to begin its descent of over 200ft by 21 locks to the Wigan basin. On each lock look for the enamelled plate carrying the Arabic figures which

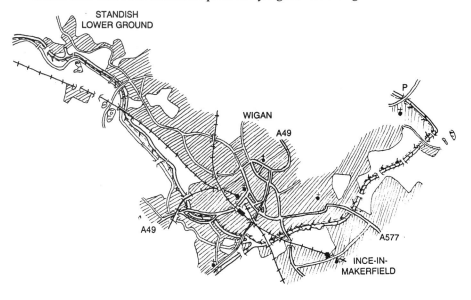

Wigan - Trencherfield Mill from the Wigan Pier Exhibition

Lock numbering at Wigan

gives its place in order from Leeds. Below each plate, cut into the stone, Roman figures give the lock's position in the flight. The area around the top lock is cobbled and behind the Waterways Office you can see the remains of old stabling for the horses.

Pass Withington Lane Bridge (58), where you are 90 miles from Leeds and 37 from Liverpool. At Cale Lane Bridge (57) you pass the Commercial Inn. Look for the date 1816, the figures cut into the stone on either side of the keystone of the bridge. Beside the towpath grow elderberry, guelder rose, hawthorn, rose and blackthorn, all heavily laden with fruit. Alder, willow, white popular, birch and cherry flourish too. Beneath the trees look for figwort and scentless mayweed.

Pass Kirkless Hall Bridge (56) and, beyond, the distinctive black and white Kirkless Hall public house. From here you can now see the skyline of Wigan with its towering flats and offices, much changed from its heavily industrialised era. At lock 9, on the far bank, a long slag-heap, thrown up by the coal and iron works, has been retained. Today vegetation softens its outline and scattered over it are circular moulds of clinker from the ovens. Climb to the top for a spectacular panoramic view, which includes all Saints church with its "leaning" spire.

Return to the towpath and stroll the now pleasingly paved way. Very few traces remain of the old collieries, such as Rose Bridge at the twelfth lock, that lined the waterway. Some are replaced by smart new factories or their sites have been grassed over and many young trees thrive. Pass St Patrick's Rugby League football ground. Continue by the Shepherds Arms at the much widened Britannia Bridge (53). Stroll the attractive towpath, where on the opposite bank stands the huge Girobank building with its pleasing seats and landscaped grounds. Then on the far bank you can see the start of the Leigh Branch. This branch continues eastwards through reclaimed and landscaped land. In Leigh the canal becomes the Bridgewater Canal, giving access to Manchester.

Beyond Chapel Lane Bridge (52), on the opposite bank, a new conference complex has replaced the old waterways repair works. Beside it is a dry dock and behind this you can see a Victorian cotton mill with two splendid chimneys. A few yards on beside the towpath are waterside gardens and the massive Trencherfield Mill, once a spinning and weaving mill. In the Machine Hall on the ground floor stands the world's largest working steam engine (2500hp). Today it is steamed daily and provides central heating for the vast complex. Also on the same floor you can see the various machines used in spinning cotton, colliery fans and engines, and a rope walk. Above, the other floors are in use.

From here a glass-sided wide boat takes you on a short journey along the canal basin, under the Pottery Changeline Bridge (51), past the Terminal Warehouse built in 1777 and so named from the days when the canal ended here, to the Heritage Centre at Wigan Pier. Here, housed in two carefully restored old warehouses built around 1890, is The Way We Were exhibition, which spans the years 1890 to 1914. There is also the unusual combination of museum exhibits and live theatre. The entrance fee includes a visit to the mill, the water bus and Wigan Pier and is very worthwhile.

The pier, and many more along the Leeds and Liverpool Canal, served as landing stages for loading and unloading coal, serving various coal mines. Wigan pier stood opposite today's Heritage Centre. In the 1930s George Orwell, Wigan's famous writer, could not find the pier when he wrote his book *The Road to Wigan Pier*. He decided that it had never existed. It had, but had been dismantled in 1929. In 1984 local college students made a full-scale replica as part of the new developments and this is what you can see.

The joke about Wigan Pier, some 15 miles from the sea, was spread by George Formby, father of the comedian, who lived a mile from the gantry. The Wiganers loved the joke. It was a way of making fun of the better-off folk who could take holidays at Southport and other seaside resorts which had pleasure piers.

Here you can walk both sides of the canal; on the towpath to see the pier and along the opposite bank through pretty gardens with many artefacts of the canal age and information panels. Continue along the towpath, now moving out into a more rural area where the canal margins have been invaded by a vast growth of arrowheads. Stride on past Pagefield Lock (88), built in 1904 because of subsidence in the canal bed caused by mining. Look left to see the River Douglas once again, almost hidden from view by alders and reeds. Great pools have formed in areas of subsidence and these support vast stands of bulrushes. Continue past Ell Meadow Locks (89), a pair side by side - one out of use - where the canal drops 6ft 6in.

Pass under Marland Mill Bridge (49) and Grimshaws Bridge (48). Look for a horse pull-out here. It is sometimes called a "dog wash" but was constructed so that any horse which fell into the canal could be rescued. Further on the canal narrows, the only evidence of Crooke Lock, made obsolete by subsidence. As you near the village of Crooke, look for an inlet to the old John Pit, where 7ft-long boats fetching coal were "legged" to and from the coal face. Now it provides cosy moorings for several boats.

Follow the curving canal past more moorings to Crooke Bridge (47), which you cross. Here stands Crooke Hall, an attractive and welcoming waterside public house.

There is a choice of route for your return. Either retrace your steps or walk through the nicely restored pit village (only one road) to turn right at the end. Cross the road and catch a bus from opposite the Royal Oak to Wigan bus station. A second bus from here will take you out to the Crown Hotel at New Springs. With good luck this should take about three-quarters of an hour. (For information, phone 0161 228 7811.)

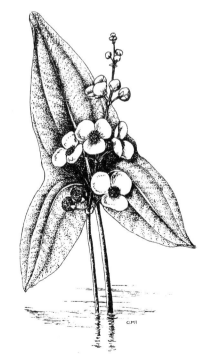

Arrowhead

129

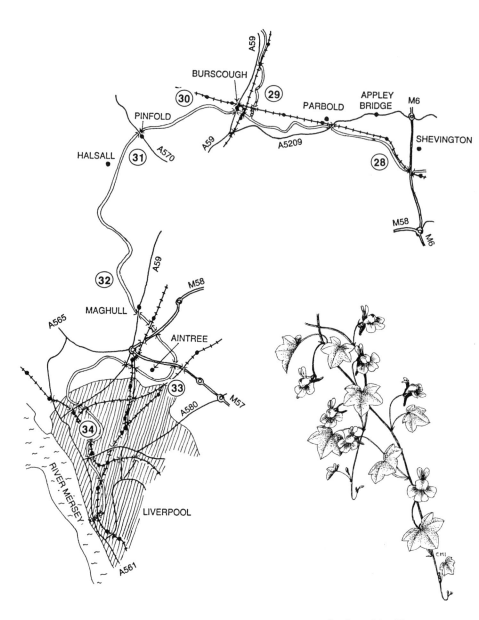

Ivy-leaved toadflax

Walk 28: Circular walk from Crooke via Parbold

Distance:	11 miles
Time:	6 hours
Maps:	OS Pathfinder 711 SD 40/50 Wigan & Ormskirk
	699 SD 41/51 Chorley & Burscough Bridge
Terrain:	Easy walking all the way.

Park in the car park of the canalside Crooke Hall public house in the village of Crooke. The landlord welcomes walkers but asks that you let him know you are leaving your car. The village, newly renovated, was once a pit village and gets its name from the bend in the River Douglas which flows parallel with the canal. The Douglas was used for transportation, linking Wigan with the Irish Sea, before the canal was cut. It was known as the River Douglas Navigation. In 1720 it was improved to transport coal and stone but very soon colliery owners wanted even better transportation and decided on an artificial waterway following the route of the river. Today the Douglas is a narrow meandering brook and nearly all trace of its earlier busy days has gone.

Cross Crooke Bridge (47) and walk, with the canal to your right, along the towpath through delightful countryside. Great reed mace and great reed grow along the banks and from dense oak woodland fly jays that have been feeding on the plenteous acorns. Continue past alder-lined banks to pass the Navigation Inn. At Gathurst Bridge (46), which carries the B5206, three forms of transport converge, the canal, the Wigan to Stockport railway and the M6, the latter carried on a lofty bridge overtopping the railway.

Beyond is a side-by-side double lock, Deans, where the canal descends 6ft 9in. Close by is the lock keeper's cottage and the area has been pleasingly cobbled. Coal from Orrell was brought down by tramway and loaded here. Today the lock down into the River Douglas Navigation is boarded up. Swans, grey wagtails and a heron can all be seen.

Stroll on to Pass Fisher's (45) and then Ranicar's swing bridge (44), both locked open. Ivy-leaved toadflax flowers in the crevices of the stone supports. Continue past Finch Mill swing bridge (43) where, in

Windmill, Parbold

the wall just before the bridge, remnants of iron piping remind you that factories once lined the banks. Where a carpet mill once stood white poplars, willows and hawthorn now stand.

And then the waterside way takes you under Appley Bridge (42) and past a row of attractive cottages. To your left the land slopes gently upwards towards Beacon Park. The modern industry along the banks is well screened by lofty trees and the towpath is attractively landscaped. At Appley locks (91) the deep one is the original. It was by-passed later by two shallower ones to save water. They lower the canal by 12ft and as you are now virtually at sea level these are the last locks you will pass before reaching Liverpool. Here you might encounter the Rose of Parbold, a wide boat, run by a trust of the same name to take youngsters with physical disabilities and learing difficulties for trips.

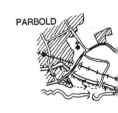

Stroll the lovely way, with a glimpse of Ashurst's Beacon high on its hill. Pass under Hand Lane Bridge (41) and Gillibrand Bridge (40), where a kingfisher is often seen. The canal along this reach shares the valley with the railway. To the right you can see the two splendid spires of churches at Parbold. Pass Chapel House Bridge (39), where there was once a brewery, and walk on towards Parbold. Beyond Alder Lane Bridge (38) the canal swings sharp left. Here look for a short cut which was the start of a link to the Ribble - but it remained just a short cut.

Ahead is Parbold Bridge (37) and beyond, on the left, the stump of an old windmill, now housing a dress shop. Much flour was milled at Parbold and today the old mill that stood on the far bank has been replaced by elegant, attractive town houses. Here leave the canal and turn left to walk along Mill Lane, past the Windmill public house. Turn left onto Alder Lane by the Stocks Tavern. Cross the busy road with care and take the first right turn, Bradshaw Lane.

Continue along the hedged way, beyond the houses, and where it swings right take the footpath, signposted Chapel House. Walk ahead along the stiled way, over a footbridge, and then left by a track. Look for a cross enclosed by railings. Here stood the old Douglas Chapel, erected in 1526, rebuilt in 1621 and demolished in 1875. Continue over the cobbled yard to rejoin the canal at bridge 39, passed earlier on your way to Parbold. Walk on, now with the canal to your left, to cross bridge 40. Climb the cobbled way through woodland where long tailed tits flit. Ignore the stile to the left. Cross the railway bridge and at the T-junction of tracks turn right to pass two houses.

Take the easy-to-miss continuing footpath on the right, which leads into, and then out of, woodland. Climb the slope, with trees continuing on your left. Look right for a good view of Ashurst's Beacon. Stride on to a stile to a road. Cross and walk on beside the straggly hawthorns and a fence to your left. Go on, with woodland to your right, to take a stile halfway along a fence, below a large ash tree. Continue to a heavily wooded gill and take the left of two stiles. Drop down steps to cross a footbridge into Fairy Glen. Climb the steps beyond, and turn right. Just before the farm take a stile on your left.

Walk ahead to a gap in the hedge in the far corner. Cross a track and continue straight ahead over a field where a sparrowhawk glides low. Cross another lane, turn right and then almost immediately left to continue in the same general direction to the B5373. Cross the road and

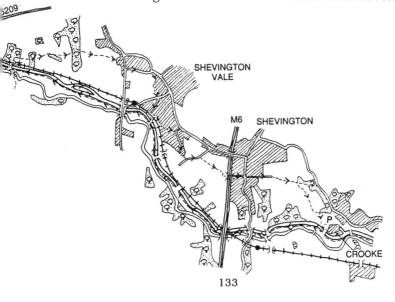

Parbold

walk right to pass a small postbox. Beyond, take the signposted track off left, which passes the backs of houses. Where the track divides take the lower one. Continue where the unmade way becomes tree-lined and walk to where it is metalled. Turn sharp right into a waymarked road and, where it swings left, turn right to take an unsignposted way into woodland. At the fence bear right down steps to peer through great steel barred gates onto a large flooded gravel pit. Ignore the footbridge and stroll on the lovely way, with a pretty brook to your left, to the road.

Cross and turn left. Stride to a signposted way, going off right, to walk between houses of a large housing estate. Just before the railway line, walk left to a cul-de-sac. Bear left, climbing a narrow path through a grassy area. Cross the road and take the right of two tracks, past more houses to another road. Turn right and walk past a terrace of older houses to the end of the road. Turn left and walk in front of another terrace to take the stone signposted footpath on the right by the last house. Follow the delightful path with glorious views down into the Douglas valley. At the next stile, walk left along a metalled road for 100yds. Look for a grassy track right leading to a sturdy stile onto the golf course.

From the stile walk ahead, with the hedge to the left, keeping a wary eye for golf balls, and continue to cross a bridge over the M6. Beyond, walk on along a path to join Vicarage Lane, which rapidly moves out into country. Keep straight on with the ICI works, suitably screened, to your right. Stride the good way. Ignore the stile on the left and continue to the green at Crooke to rejoin your car.

Through the grassy gap between the houses wagons once brought coal from John Pit and Taylor Pit to waiting barges on the canal.

Junction Bridge, where the Rufford Branch leaves the canal near Burscough

Walk 29: Circular walk from Parbold

Distance:	10¹/₂ miles
Time:	5-6 hours
Map:	OS Pathfinder 699 SD 41/51 Chorley and Burscough Bridge
Terrain:	Easy walking.

Park in the village of Parbold close to the canal. Continue on the towpath, which is on the opposite bank to the old brick windmill - a reminder that the village was once a centre for flour milling. Water lilies spread their leaves over the waterway to your left and large clumps of Canadian pondweed float near the surface.

Pass over an aqueduct high above the fast-flowing River Douglas. Now the flat countryside stretches away for as far as the eye can see and in one vast field long rows of Brussels sprouts grow. Lapwings and common gulls feed in a cleared potato field and a flock of young long-tailed tits hurries ahead through hawthorns along the bank.

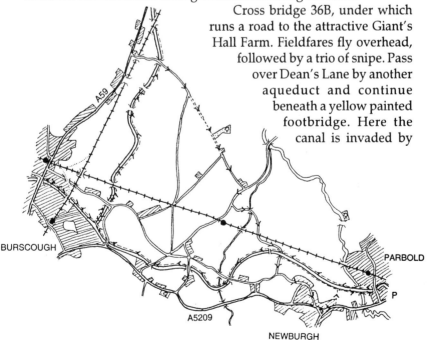

Cross bridge 36B, under which runs a road to the attractive Giant's Hall Farm. Fieldfares fly overhead, followed by a trio of snipe. Pass over Dean's Lane by another aqueduct and continue beneath a yellow painted footbridge. Here the canal is invaded by masses of arrowheads, a plant with arrow-shaped leaves. On either side, well screened, are two treatment works. Stride on past Spencer's swing bridge (36) and look for a large field of weed-free grass to be sold as turf. Here you are 101 miles from Leeds and 26 from Liverpool.

Look for the small aqueduct (35A) over the very narrow River Tawd. Drop down the bank to see the ornate keystone, dated 1838. Stroll on the lovely way to pass under Moss Bridge (35) to pass, on either bank, West Lancashire tree nursery, where grow an enormous variety of shrubs, bushes and forest trees. By the next bridge (34) is the Ring-o'-Bells public house, the same name as the bridge. There is a mooring here and once it was a boatmen's community.

Cross the aqueduct high above the Eller Brook and stroll on to Glovers swing bridge (33). Look here for a flock of Dorset Horn sheep. The ram has huge curling horns. Then you reach Junction Bridge (1), built in 1816, the first on the Rufford Branch. The branch was designed to take Mersey flat boats and to link the mainline with the River Douglas and the the Ribble.

Here picturesque cottages line a small green and a dry dock. Stand on the imposing arched bridge for a delightful view of the branch line winding deep into the fertile, gently sloping countryside. Along the Rufford branch is your return route, but first continue along the mainline towpath towards Burscough. Look for a large planting of everlasting flowers and then walk on to pass the pleasant Burscough grain mill on the far bank, the red brick building a good foil for the autumn colouring of the trees that grow around it.

Pass under the railway bridge (32B) and onto Burscough Bridge (32A) to leave the canal to visit the small agricultural town. Long distance boatmen lived here, many manning fly-boats. These had the right of way on the water and made great speed carrying

Burscough Grain Mill

perishable goods to market.

Return along the canal to cross the magnificent bridge at the start of the Rufford branch and walk left to pass the Latham locks (1-2). Continue below Runnel Brow Bridge (2), with its lock (3) just beyond. Look for large clumps of the pretty corn marigolds in among rows of leeks. Stroll on beneath bridge 2A, which carries the railway. The towpath passes through a narrow arch. Continue on the wide grassy way, which is a joy to walk. Beyond Moss lock (4) look for dragonflies darting along the waterside vegetation.

Next you pass German's lock (5), close to German's Bridge (3), and then Chicken lock (6) and Baldwins Bridge (4), all set in tranquil countryside. At Prescott Bridge (5) a water vole swims fast across the cut. Here there are picnic tables. Leave the branchline and turn right to walk a quiet hedged lane. Cross a bridge over the very long straight Wham ditch. Ignore the footpath on the left and continue to where the road swings right. Stride ahead along a signposted stiled track. Carry on beside birch woodland and then an extensive field of onions to come to Wood Lane.

Walk straight on, with fields of cabbages, and then potatoes, on either side. At the T-junction turn right along Hoscar Moss Road. Take the first left turn into Dean's Lane, which is lined with maize. Ignore Frog Lane and walk on. Cross the narrow River Tawd and then, with care, the railway line. Go on under the aqueduct crossed earlier, the road pleasingly flagged and cobbled. Walk on along the lane to turn left into Back Lane and on past fields of strawberries. Join the A5209 to walk into Newburgh. As you pass the village green, look for the old market cross and a pump, beneath magnificent beeches.

Hurry on along the A class road and then leave it at a signposted left turn beyond a cottage called Wayside and opposite Greenhill Farm. Follow the grassy track, which drops downhill between fields of Brussels sprouts and potatoes to the side of the canal on the opposite bank to the towpath. Turn right to walk between enormous stands of great reed, 10ft high, to come to the windmill at Parbold. Cross the canal bridge to rejoin your car.

Water vole swimming

The Greater Manchester Hide at Martin Mere, with pinkfooted geese flying in

Walk 30: Circular walk from Burscough

Distance:	9¹/₂ miles
Time:	5 hours
Map:	OS Pathfinder 698 SD 21/31 Southport
	699 SD 41/51 Chorley & Burscough Bridge
Terrain:	Easy walking.

Park in one of the free car parks in Burscough that lie close to the canal. This small agricultural town has interesting shops in which to linger. Join the canal at Burscough Bridge (32A) and walk, with the canal to your left, towards Liverpool. Very soon you leave the houses behind as you stroll out into the pleasing countryside. On the far side great reed, 10ft tall, colonises the bank and has invaded the water. Ash, laden with huge bunches of papery keys, and hawthorn, heavily berried, line the towpath.

Continue past moorings and then on to Crabtree swing bridge (32) beside the Latham Slipway public house. To your right look for lapwings and starlings feeding in fields where the green sprouts of winter wheat are coming through. At New Lane swing bridge (31) you pass the Farmers Arms. Carry on past a row of pretty cottages, with grassy fronts running down to the water's edge. Here red admiral butterflies and speckled woods flit about the flowers.

Go on past Great Score swing bridge (30), which carries a footpath. Beyond stretches a vast field of

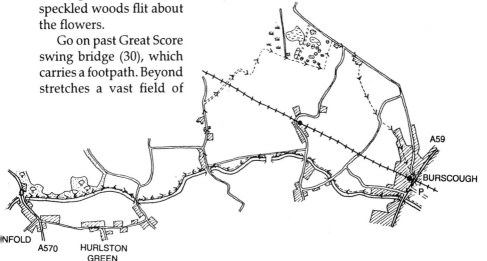

A59

BURSCOUGH
P

NFOLD
A570   HURLSTON
        GREEN

Lone cottage at start of walk

celery, which fills the air with its attractive smell. Martin Lane Bridge (29) comes next and all around the fields stretch away into the misty distance, with just enough trees and hedges to make it a delightful flatland. Along the towpath red campion and pink convolvulus flower and a heron wings its way towards Heaton's Bridge. Beside the bridge (28) stands a public house. Evan Heaton was a yeoman farmer whose fields were separated by the cutting of the canal.

Stride on along the peaceful towpath which is soon to be shadowed by the woodland of Scarisbrick Hall. (Now you are 106 miles from Leeds and 21 from Liverpool.) The glorious trees, particularly beautiful in autumn, stretch all the way to Scarisbrick Bridge (27A). At this bridge packet boat passengers, on holiday, alighted to take a horse-drawn carriage to Southport. They refreshed themselves at the Red Lion close by. Beyond the bridge, and on the far side, is Wheelwright's Wharf, one of the many along the canal, where night-soil from the Lancashire towns was unloaded. The manure was used to fertilise the soil of Martin Mere after it was drained.

Hidden behind the extensive woodland lies the Victorian Gothic Scarisbrook Hall, occupied by the Scarisbrook family until 1948. It is now a school, and not open to the public. Leave the canal beyond the bridge and walk for 200yds along the busy A570. On the opposite side of the road is the medieval wayside Scarisbrook Cross, cut from a single slab of stone. This is one of two lines of crosses - one leads to Ormskirk and the other to Burscough Priory. The crosses served a dual purpose, one as wayside shrines and the other as route markers over the treacherous marshy ground.

From this point there are too many busy roads to complete a fully circular walk, so return along the towpath of the canal to pass Heaton's

Bridge (28). Go on to leave the cut at Martin Lane Bridge (29). Walk north along Martin Lane to pass a huge field of lettuces. Beyond the Martin Inn, walk on along the continuing narrow Martin Lane to pass a house built in 1741 - and more lettuces. Then you come to acres of glasshouses and, when you are halfway along these, take a good track leading off right. Cross the railway track with care and stroll on to an old corrugated iron shed where you follow the track right, passing through broccoli and Brussels sprouts and then beetroot. At a ditch, follow the waymarked track left. Beyond the stile walk on to a gate. Pass through and turn right to cross Boat House sluice and continue walking beside the perimeter fence of Martin Mere. Follow the track left to continue to Fish Lane.

To visit Martin Mere, the wildfowl and wetlands centre, turn left. (For details phone 01704 895181). To visit Mere Sands Wood nature Reserve and to continue the walk, turn right and go on along Fish Lane. To your left stands the picturesque ruinous Tarlscough Hall. Carry on to pass Brandreth Barn, on the right side of the road, and turn immediately right by its boundary wall. (For Mere Sands continue to Curlew Farm and turn left; for details phone 01704 821809.) The rather indistinct but waymarked track crosses between rows of potatoes from where partridges take off. Aim for the right end of a straggly hedge to pick up a cart track which continues in the same direction. Look for the pretty large-flowered hemp-nettle growing here.

Press on along the road and take a short footpath continuing in the same general direction. At the next road, Moss Nook, still walk ahead. At the end, turn right and go along Redcat Lane. Turn right onto the A59 and cross the railway to rejoin your car. The canal lies further along the A class road.

Partridges

143

Walk 31: Circular walk from Scarisbrook Bridge via Downholland

Distance:	9 miles
Time:	4-5 hours
Maps:	OS Pathfinder 698 SD 21/31 Southport
	710 SD 20/30 Formby and Maghull
Terrain:	Easy walking.

P ark in the very large yard of the Red Lion public house, which lies close to Scarisbrook Bridge (27A) on the edge of the village of Pinfold. The landlord welcomes walkers; he asks that you let him know you have left your car. Turn right out of the yard and walk 400yds along the A570, below a row of horse-chestnut trees. To your right lies a vast field of leeks and beyond stands a row of Lombardy poplars.

Turn right into Pinfold Lane, where once an enclosure stood for collecting stray cattle. Stride on past a thatched cottage before moving out into quiet countryside, where fields of cabbages stretch away into the distance. After 800yds, take the footpath on your left, signposted Primrose Hill. To your left oak and sycamore shadow a hedged ditch where blackberries and elderberries grow. Ignore the footbridge on your left and continue on, making detours to the right of small water-filled hollows, edged with trees, from which clay was removed.

Continue where, on either side, large quantities of potatoes have been harvested. The bare earth now supports red dead-nettle, shepherd's purse, chickweed, scentless mayweed, pink persicaria and groundsel - all in flower. Descend with care the steep-sided ditch that stretches across the field, cutting across the right of way, and dig your toes well in to the soft brown soil as you clamber up the other side. Keep to the left of the electricity substation and continue to a track, where

Cutting - Halsall Hill Bridge in the distance

144

you walk on to Primrose Hill Farm on Asmall Lane. Cross, and continue on along Cut Lane, a quiet tarmacked way which passes between stubble fields, pink with the pretty weed - common fumitory. From here you have your first view of Ormskirk church, with its separate spire and tower. It is believed that originally it had only a spire and a tower was added to house the bells from Burscough Priory. Stroll on through the market garden of West Lancashire, where to your left lie gently rolling pastures with hedgerows and pockets of woodland, and to your right stretch acres of flat land. Ignore the footpath on your left and continue to where the lane swings sharp right. Here go ahead, climbing steadily to walk to the right of the wall of Clieves Hills Farm. Follow the track as it swings right to join Narrow Lane, Clieves Hills, where you turn left.

145

Walk on along the continuing Fir Tree Lane (part of the Lancashire Cycle Way). Stride on along the lane - where no fir trees are to be seen - to turn right into Clieves Hills Lane.

Carry on where it swings left and climb past Landmark Cottage and then to the viewpoint on Clieves Hills, 590ft above sea level. Sit on one of the seats to enjoy the fabulous view of the Catholic cathedral at Liverpool, Snowdon, Anglesey, Formby Point and Blackpool Tower. Press on, now downhill, to Formby Lane, where you cross and walk left. Pass a house named The Old Waggoners and then turn right beyond, to walk a signposted track to Walsh Hall stables. Bear right and then left between the outbuildings. Turn right before the fence and climb a stile obscured by a large sycamore. Stride across a pasture to a stile with a white-painted top rail and cross the footbridge beyond. Stride ahead over a very large stubble field to cross Rimmer's swing bridge (20) over the canal. Turn right to walk the towpath, which is lined with hawthorn beneath which figwort flowers.

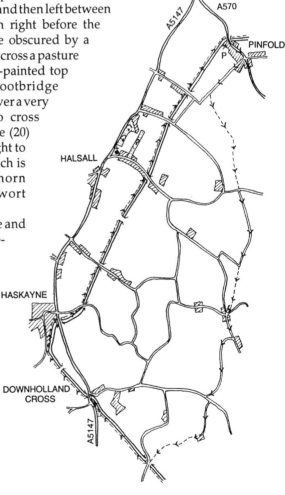

The towpath is wide and grassy and on the opposite bank grow vast stands of great reed. Pass a large winding hole and then a milepost indicating 16 miles to Liverpool. Away to the right you can see Tanpit Farm, where hides would have been tanned. Scarisbrook Hotel is passed just before Downholland Bridge (20A), which carries Mairscough Lane. Enjoy the pleasing

146

Pair of green woodpeckers

seats on either side of the bridge - just right for your picnic. Go on to pass the attractive Downholland Hall and its accompanying swing bridge (21). Beyond, the towpath has been reinforced and covered with sand, making it a pleasure to walk. Look left to see a thatched cottage. Pass under Haskayne Bridge (21A), which carries Delf Lane, and then long-term moorings.

Ship Bridge (22) comes next, with more seats and a public house of the same name alongside. Pass under Harker's Bridge (23), a pleasing stone bridge reinforced with iron supports. Then the canal enters a cutting through rock, the left side walled and railed, over which lean trees. The far bank is clad with oaks now in yellow leaf. Look for a kingfisher and a pair of green woodpeckers in the trees. Then you reach the milepost indicating 109 miles to Leeds. Nearby on November 5, 1770 Charles Mordaunt cut the first sod on this part of the canal. This is a glorious stretch of the waterway, frequented by anglers who appreciate the shelter and the quiet.

Next comes Halsall Hill Bridge (24), pleasingly cobbled where it carries a track. Pass another winding hole. Away to the left you have a good view of the church of St Cuthbert, on a rocky outcrop at Halsall. This is believed to be the oldest church building in Lancashire, parts of it dating back to 1290.

The Saracen's Head public house stands adjacent to a canal wharf and warehouse and by Halsall Warehouse Bridge (25). The large number of inns along the water in West Lancashire must have been a great comfort to the boatmen. In summer they were able to quench their thirst after the hard work of opening the heavy swing bridges. In winter they would have enjoyed a cosy evening stop or a welcome break on tedious packet journeys.

Pass under Hulme's Bridge (26) and continue to Weavers Bridge (27). Climb the steps just before Scarisbrook Bridge (27A), turn right to cross the canal and walk on to rejoin your car in the yard of the Red Lion.

St Andrew's Church, Maghull, with Unsworth Chapel

Walk 32: Circular walk from Downholland via Maghull

Distance:	8¹/₂ miles
Time:	4-5 hours
Map:	OS Pathfinder 710 SD 20/30 Formby and Maghull
Terrain:	Easy walking.

Park on the grass verge at the canal end of Green's Lane, close to Rimmer's Bridge (20). To reach this quiet corner of West Lancashire, approach from Ormskirk via Formby Lane; or from Downholland Cross, using Mairscough Lane, then Hall and Eager Lanes. If coming from Lydiate, use the Southport Road and then Hall and Eager Lanes.

From the verge on the north-east side of the canal, walk across Rimmer's swing bridge and continue along Eager Lane. Turn right into Hall Lane and continue past the old school, now a private house. Turn left at the footpath sign for Lollies Bridge. Follow the white-topped posts ahead, along the field edge and then to the right of an oak hedge. Cross a former racecourse track by stiles and follow the waymarks to bear right to cross a second track by two stiles. Stride on, with a fence to your right, to another stile beyond an oak tree to come to Lydiate Hill Bridge (18). Descend the steps before the bridge and stroll right along the towpath, where wild parsley is in flower.

Pass under Lollies Bridge (17A), which carries the A5147, and continue along the delightful way. A pair of grey wagtails flits from stone to stone along the reinforced edge of the waterway. Pass under Dicconson's Bridge (17) and climb the steps beyond to Pilling Lane, where you walk left. Blackbirds feast on the berry-laden hawthorn bushes lining the way. Go on beyond Berry's Farm and turn left off the lane to take the public footpath to Altcar Lane. To your left, alders edge a narrow ditch, and to your right stretches a large field from which a flock of fieldfare takes off.

Cross Altcar Lane and walk left. At Crisp's Farm notice the red sandstone

House dated 1596

149

flags used for fencing. In the bushes about the yard a flock of house sparrows flies off with a sparrowhawk in close pursuit. Opposite the farmyard stands an attractive red brick house with the date 1596 on it. At the sharp bend, left, in the lane, turn right to walk into the charming Mercer Court, where more sandstone flags have been used for fencing. Bear right to pass in front of The Byre; the barn to your left is dated 1694. Bear right along a reinforced track and then left beyond a gate. Walk to a track edging a field, where you turn right to stride on to join the Cheshire Lines path.

Turn left onto a reinforced track that forms part of the Trans Pennine Trail and follows the trackbed of the former Southport and Cheshire Lines extension railway, which stopped carrying passengers in 1952.

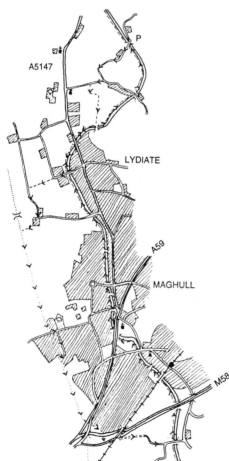

Stride on through productive farmland and continue on the waymarked track until the tarmac ends. Then walk on along a narrow path, with willow woodland to the left.

Where the track is blocked by the embankment of the B5422, walk left for 100yds. Join the B road and cross it carefully. Continue along The Old Racecourse Road, with Lawson Marden works to your right. Stride on to a right turn named Mead Way and follow it until it ends in a cul-de-sac. On the right railed steps enable you to rejoin the trackbed of the dismantled railway. Go on along the bush-lined way. To your left lie the houses on the outskirts of Maghull and to your right rough pastures stretch away. Cross the River Alt on a high-level bridge to pass through a signposted kissing gate on the side of the A59, now a dual carriageway.

It is difficult to cross here and stride on the continuing footpath, so turn left and walk to the traffic lights. Cross and turn right to walk along the opposite pavement to the gap in the fencing of the dual carriageway. Follow the clear path beside Dover's Brook and, where it winds left, walk ahead to pass below a section of the M58. Press on along the continuing fenced path to cross another section of the motorway by a footbridge. Turn left and follow the reinforced track to pass below the railway line.

Head on along the wide grassy track, which bisects a large ploughed field. Look here for vast numbers of the pretty field pansy growing in the furrows. Keep to the left of Wood Hall Farm and follow the lane beyond, as it swings right and joins Brewery Lane. From here you have a first pleasing view of Melling Church. Turn left and pass a short row of cottages, to take a gate on the left. Stride the access track beyond to the side of the canal, north of Melling Stone Bridge (11), where stone from Melling Delph quarry was loaded onto barges.

Walk left along the towpath, with fields of winter wheat on either side of the waterway. Pass under the motorway bridge and then the railway bridge (11A). Here black-headed gulls in winter plumage preen on the water and more feed on a sports field to the left. The canal narrows where once it was crossed by a swing bridge and now by Draper's Bridge (11B), a high footbridge. Pass Maghull Hall swing bridge (12), which carries a narrow road. Stroll on the quiet, seemingly rural way. This is a lovely stretch of the towpath, with double-sided seats and a grand view across a meadow to St Andrew's, the 19th-century parish church of Maghull.

At Northway Bridge (12A) leave the towpath by steps on the far side. Cross the A59 with great care to walk left. Descend steps into the churchyard of St Andrew's. At the bottom of the steps, under a huge beech, look for the ornate tombstone of Frank Hornby, the inventor of meccano, who died in 1936. Close by is the 13th-century Unsworth Chapel, all that remains of a much earlier church. Walk round the gracious St Andrew's. Sadly all the doors are locked because of earlier theft.

Leave by the steps and retrace your way to the towpath and walk on. Pass under Red Lion Bridge (13). You are now in the centre of this pleasant town, once an agricultural village. In 1827 the packet fare along the canal for a sick woman to be carried from Maghull to Wigan for treatment was 1s 10d.

Stride on to Shaw's swing bridge (14), where innumerable ducks and geese congregate. Close by is Maghull library and a row of convenient shops. Pass under a road bridge and continue on to the Methodist swing bridge (15). Between this bridge and the next, Running Horse Bridge (16), a culvert beneath the canal carries the brook that marks the boundary between Lydiate and Maghull. In 1994 the culvert collapsed and the wall of the canal was breached, causing severe flooding. The level of the canal dropped all the way to Liverpool.

Go on past the Running Horse public house and the remnants of works on the far bank that once made metal containers. The site is now part of a housing project. Beyond a large winding hole, pass under bridge

17, where you left the canal earlier. Press on along the glorious way to pass under Lollies Bridge and on to Lydiate Hill Bridge (18). Here notice the marks made by masons on the stonework of the arch.

The quiet way continues past another winding hole and on towards Jackson's Bridge (19). Look here for a kingfisher flying fast towards the bridge. Beyond, it flies from one side of the waterway to the other and then is lost to sight. Stride on to Rimmer's swing bridge, which you cross to rejoin your car.

Azolla - the water fern

Walk 33: Circular walk from Stone Bridge, Melling, via Netherton

Distance:	5¹/₂ miles
Time:	3 hours
Maps:	OS Pathfinder 710 SD 20/30 Formby and Maghull
	721 SJ 29/39 Wallasey
Terrain:	Easy walking.

Park in a layby in Brewery Lane on the west side of Melling Stone Bridge (11). Walk west, away from the canal, to take the signposted track, where the lane turns sharp left. Continue ahead to pass Wood Hall Farm, walk towards the end of walk 32. Follow the cobbled way, left, beyond the barn, where geese on the farm pond warn of intruders. Stride over the wild grassy way, which bisects a huge field where the delicate field pansy grows in profusion. Pass under the railway bridge ahead.

Go along the reinforced track, left, to cross the bridge over a section of the M58. Carry on along the fenced path through rough ground to pass below a second section of the motorway. Stroll on beside the narrow Dover's Brook to the side of the A59, here a dual carriageway with crash barriers. The continuing signposted footpath is on the opposite side of the road. To avoid a difficult crossing, walk right to cross at the traffic lights (500yds), returning on the footpath on the west side of the very busy road.

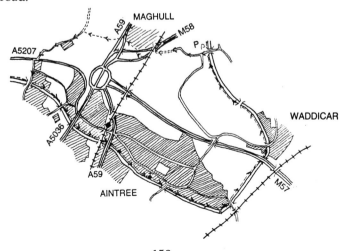

Melling Church

Pass through the signposted gate to walk the footpath, with the fast-flowing River Alt channelled in a deep gutter to your right. Pass under the pedestrian arch of a bridge which once carried the Cheshire Lines railway and is now a traffic-free path for walkers, cyclists and people with physical disabilities. Stride on along the raised bank, with ploughed fields to your left and the river to your right. Look for tansy, a bright yellow flower, along the side of the path. At Mill Dam footbridge, turn left and stroll the reinforced track towards a farm. Beyond you can see the spire of Sefton church. Join the hedged Chapel Lane, where you walk right, continuing to the Northern Perimeter Road at Netherton.

Cross the busy road with care and walk on along the continuing Chapel lane. Pass St Benet's Catholic church and then beside the pleasing Netherton Green on your right. Carry on along Aldrins Lane and, before Netherton swing bridge (6), turn left to join the towpath.

Here in autumn, for several years, the waterway has been densely covered with azolla, a foreign weed believed to have come from a fish tank. You can see little water but the weed does not deter the mallards and moorhens who seem to have started their courtship rituals. Yellow water lilies still survive among the tightly packed green and brown mat of small serrated-edged leaves, but the pads of the lilies are small.

Stroll on where houses, lining both sides of the canal, are well screened by reeds, sedges, poplars, elderberry and hawthorns. Continue beside a milestone, which tells you that you are 8 miles from Liverpool

Kestrel hovering

and 119¹/₄ from Leeds. As you pass beneath Dunning's Bridge (7A), which carries the A5036, look ahead for a charming rural view. Emerging from the bridge you can see that beyond the forest trees and bushes there are works and houses. A pair of grey wagtails runs nimbly along the edging stones of the cut, with heads and necks dipping at every step.

Bridge 7C carries Mersey Rail to Old Roan station and then comes Old Road Bridge (7D), which carries the A59. Beyond elegant willows and great clumps of shrubs more houses and industry are well screened. Next comes Blue Anchor Bridge (8) and beyond you can see Aintree racecourse on the right. Here more reeds and sedges line the way and in autumn their leaves are papery-yellow. Look for the large winding hole gradually being encroached by the reeds.

The canal then makes its famous turn and you come to the narrow Handcock's swing bridge. It carries traffic, so cross with care. A hovering kestrel drops suddenly to a field to your left. There are more fields to the far side of the waterway. Cross the River Alt. Now scattered thorn bushes and yellowing birch cover the rough pasture on either bank.

The bridge carrying the M57 comes next. Just before you reach Ledson's swing bridge you can see, on the far bank, the Horse and Jockey public house. Another road bridge crosses the canal and once under you pass the BICC works to your right. It stands on the site of Melling Pottery, which operated from the 19th century. It made stoneware pottery for jam. Then you have your first glimpse of Melling church.

The towpath now leads you out into the rural depths of West Lancashire. Pass Holmes swing bridge (10) and follow the curving canal into peaceful agricultural land. Pass another winding hole, beyond which stands the pleasing Melling church, across the fields. Stone from Melling Delph quarry was loaded onto barges near here. Loading bays were located close by, allowing narrow boats to turn round. Walk on to pass below Melling Stone Bridge (11), where all trace of the weed azolla has gone. Turn left and follow the Waterways access track to Brewery Lane to rejoin your car.

Stanley Dock, Liverpool

Walk 34: Linear walk from Netherton to the end of the canal

Distance:	7¹/₂ miles
Time:	3-4 hours
Map:	OS Pathfinder 721 SJ 29/39 Wallasey
Terrain:	Easy walking. All gates open and therefore easy access to and from the towpath.

This walk along the final stretch of the towpath is linear. On such a walk the return to the start poses a problem. You could walk back along the towpath. Or perhaps a friend with a car might meet you and drive you back to the start. To return by train use Mersey Rail, Sandhills to Old Roan station; see text of walks 33 and 34 (for information phone 0151 709 9696). It is also possible to return by Mersey Bus, using the 137 to the city centre (Gyratory) and then by the 55 to Netherton (for information phone 0151 709 8600).

If using one or two cars, park on the south-west side of Netherton swing bridge (6) (see walk 33), which lies just off the Northern Perimeter Road. Join the towpath and walk towards Liverpool, with the canal to your left. Houses line the waterway, but banks of great reed and hedges of hawthorn soften the way. The canal itself supports a vast number of yellow water lilies. Then you pass a playing field on one side and a large

Leigh Bridge

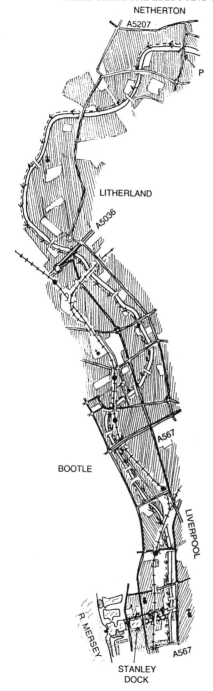

NETHERTON

A5207

P

LITHERLAND

A5036

A567

BOOTLE

LIVERPOOL

R. MERSEY

A567

STANLEY
DOCK

green on the other. Several schools are situated close by and the sound of laughing children, enjoying their playtime, fills the air.

Pass under Fleetwood's Bridge (5A) to pass more dwellings where scattered trees line the path, white dead-nettle flowers and moorhens scurry across the water to disappear under overhanging vegetation. Just before the white-painted Swift's Bridge (5) both banks of the canal have more open spaces. Next you pass a large green mound pleasingly landscaped as part of an estate. This was once an abutment of a bridge and you can see another on the opposite bank.

Look for the small $^1/_2$ mile post and several more as you continue on your way. Then a row of fine willows adorns the opposite side of the cut as you approach Gorsey Lane Bridge (4A) with, close by, the Tailor's Arms public house. As you stroll on you pass, on your right, Rimrose valley, at first hidden from view by bushes and trees. Then, when the scrub ceases, you can see open grassland, the haunt of owls and butterflies, where many wild flowers grow.

Away to the right you have your first view of the great cranes in Seaforth Dock. To your left are the houses of Litherland beyond a reed-fringed winding hole. Pied wagtails flit about the water's edge and two black-headed gulls mob a kestrel until it moves away over the continuing rough ground to the right. Among the many water-lily pads are long strands of Canadian pondweed - a plant that efficiently adds oxygen to the water.

Pass under a high footbridge (4), which has replaced a swing bridge. Here a pair of swans comes close, hoping to be fed. A flock of goldfinches takes off from leafless thorns and settles on the seed heads of dead plants in the rough pastures further from the towpath. The pleasing green way continues as industry begins to crowd both banks. You pass under another footbridge that replaced an earlier swing bridge and then a huge electricity gantry strides the waterway. Beyond you come to a wide road bridge (3) with an accompanying footbridge, followed by the Red Lion public house.

From now on the towpath is attractively landscaped. You pass under a railway bridge and then a footbridge which links old works on either bank. Look here for a large bush of wild clematis, sometimes called daddy's beard, clambering over a high fence. After a series of bridges - 2J, H, G, E and C - you continue beneath the ornate wrought-iron Litherland Road Bridge (2B). Look for the coat of arms on the far side. Walk on to pass some seats close to the site of another swing bridge, where more willows trail the far bank.

Go under the next bridge and climb the cobbled slope to your right to cross the footbridge beside the road bridge, Stanley Road Changeline Bridge (2A). Pass beneath a road bridge (1) and then a railway bridge. Look right to see an old coal wharf with the base of what was once a crane mounted on two stone plinths. Cross the next changeline footbridge (O) just before another rail bridge to regain the other side of the canal and to continue along the pleasing towpath.

Stride beneath another road (M) and footbridge with works along either side of the cut. Another footbridge passes overhead and here the towpath is bright with pink clover. Suddenly a young heron flies up from its quiet fishing and lands on the roof of a derelict building. It pauses and then wings slowly away. Some of the disused works retain their Victorian charm, with tall chimneys and canopies, one dated 1874, and it is to be hoped that these features will remain in the intense restoration that is taking place.

Go on past bracken and hawthorn on both banks, with industry beyond. A tall red brick wall supports an ornamental ivy with red and green leaves. Several rowan, maple and privet thrive, and rose bushes, laden with huge hips, grow along the edge of the towpath. Pass under another railway bridge (H), beyond which there is a seat backed by shrubs and bracken. Look across the cut to see large stands of bulrushes. As you approach a wrought-iron bridge (F), brightly painted light and

The yellow fringed water lily - rare in the north of England but abundant here near Liverpool on the canal

dark blue, look for the black iron turning post cut through by the ropes of the horses pulling the boats. On each side of the bridge a turning post protected the stonework and the ropes. Beyond are two pleasant seats and further on a large mill fronting the water.

From now on you have glimpses of the River Mersey, glinting silvery through the intervening buildings. Pass below Boundary Bridge (E), as ornate as F but not painted so dramatically. Ahead is Leigh Bridge (D), an elegant footbridge with an engraving of a heron. Beyond, the towpath is magnificently paved in keeping with the modern housing about the waterway. Next comes another sturdy bridge (C), with a roller to take the strain of the horses' ropes. Then set in the paved path is a post that tells you Leeds is 127 miles away - a dramatic moment for those who have travelled the whole distance.

Follow the towpath as it swings abruptly right, and ahead lies the impressive flight of four locks built in 1848 by Jesse Hartley, the engineer who also built Liverpool's Albert Dock. These locks lead down into Stanley Dock. Enjoy the landscaped seats. Cross the footbridge of the top lock to the other side. Drop steadily down to cross the next bridge, pass below the railway viaduct and continue to descend. Cross the waterway to continue to walk the landscaped path. Finally, through a tunnel, you can see the water of the dock. However, at the time of writing walkers could progress no farther.

Once the canal reached nearly to the Albert Dock. Over the decades short stretches have been filled in. Now it ends, like a blunt thumb, a short distance beyond the locks. To reach this point, cross the arm to Stanley Dock by the top lock footbridge and walk on to pass beneath the striking Vauxhall Bridge, refurbished in 1994. Walk on past an attractive development of houses using the pleasingly tiled towpath.

Having walked the whole length of the towpath it would be a pity to miss the view of the canal joining Stanley Dock. To do this return to Bridge C and join the road to walk left. Follow it round left along a quiet road, where you would park a second car if this was to be your method of return. Stride on to cross the busy road to Bootle (Turn right here, and then left, to reach Sandhills station, if returning by train.) Walk down Walton Street. Turn left again into Derby Road and stand on the huge bridge overlooking the dock. From here you can see the other side of the tunnel, through which flows the canal. To the left is a colonnaded warehouse. On the right stands Hartley's huge tobacco warehouse, now a listed building. Behind, completely hidden by the magnificent warehouse, is another colonnaded warehouse. Turn round and look out over the Mersey to the crenellated Victoria Tower with its six clock faces.

Liverpool - the last milepost

PRINTED BY ST EDMUNDSBURY PRESS, BURY ST EDMUNDS, SUFFOLK